Billionaire Engagement

Erica Frost

Published by Erica Frost, 2024.

Table of Contents

Chapter 1...1

Chapter 2...7

Chapter 3...13

Chapter 4...19

Chapter 5...25

Chapter 6...30

Chapter 7...35

Chapter 8...41

Chapter 9...47

Chapter 10...53

Chapter 11...59

Chapter 12...64

Chapter 13...70

Chapter 14...76

Chapter 15...81

Chapter 16...87

Chapter 17...92

Chapter 18...98

Chapter 19...104

Chapter 20...110

Chapter 21...117

Chapter 22...123

Chapter 23...130

Chapter 24...135

Chapter 25...141

Chapter 26...147

Chapter 27...153

Chapter 28...159

Bonus chapter...167

Billionaire Engagement
New Adult Boss Romance

By: Erica Frost

Foreword

Not all girls dream of falling in love. Some of us, especially those fresh out of college, just want a job. When I landed a job as PA to a Silicon Valley CEO billionaire, I thought it would be an easy ride. But instead of managing his diary, I found myself organizing his exercise regime!

Handsome yet erratic, Tate Sagarro was a nightmare as a boss. I had a business degree and yet my biggest priority was testing kale smoothies?! The man was a maniac, my complete opposite, this could never work! Before I knew it, I was pretending to be Tate's fiancé, flying to LA where I ended up naked in the pool of a famous celebrity. The craziness had to stop. The only problem was, I didn't want it to. Somehow (and I was too embarrassed to admit this), I'd fallen for Tate Sagarro.

Billionaire Engagement

Chapter 1

E vie
    It took me months to get that job.

Weeks and weeks of sitting at home, glued to the screen of my phone and my computer, waiting and praying and hoping and making all kinds of deals with the universe in a desperate attempt to get a positive response.

But, nada.

"Nobody wants you," my older brother Steve teased me when my job hunting hit the six-month mark. "You're too fat."

"I'm not fat!" I hit back, a bit self-conscious because I had actually gained some weight sitting behind the laptop, firing off emails all day, eating candy while I scrolled the job ads.

"Besides, there is no picture on my resume!"

"Maybe you sound fat?" he said, challenging me.

"And how do fat people sound?" I asked.

"Hungry!" he laughed. I had to smile at that. I knew this was Steve's clumsy way of trying to cheer me up. He had a job, working with our father in a charter boat fishing business on Lake Tahoe, taking visitors out for trout fishing in summer. It wasn't heaps of money, but enough to keep the business ticking over.

But I'd insisted on going to college, got myself a little degree to prove I was smart and that I had options besides smelling like fish all day. Only problem was, it seemed I had no options after all. Unemployment was high, the economy was slow and there were too many business graduates flooding the job market, one recruiter told me, asking if I'd be happy to work in another industry.

"Like what?" I wanted to know.

"How about accounting?" she asked.

"Err... I don't think so," I said, not wanting to mention that I had only barely passed this particular subject after several failed attempts. It also bored me to tears, and the thought of crunching numbers all day was worse than puking my guts out from motion sickness on the boat.

Then, just like that, my lucky break came.

I got a call from an agency asking me if I'd be interested in being a personal assistant.

"A PA?" I asked. "Like, a glorified secretary?"

"Nobody refers to them like that anymore," the recruiter said stiffly, clearly not impressed with my attitude.

"But I've got a degree!" I protested. "Don't PAs fetch coffee and take messages, basically?"

The problem was, I'd had this idea of me working at maybe a digital agency, or in advertising, some sort of media business, putting together witty campaigns and cute videos.

"This isn't just any PA job," the recruiter said. "Your resume was selected by Tate Sagarro."

"Who's he again?" I asked. Embarrassing moment number two. I'd heard the name but I couldn't pinpoint where. Football player maybe?

"Are you interested or not?" the recruiter asked, tetchily.

"Yes, sorry, I am."

"Google him," she said pointedly, before putting down the phone. So I did.

A picture came up of a blonde hunk with too-white teeth and hair that looked like it had more product in it than mine. He was the CEO of HumanITy, a tech start-up in Silicon Valley. It was an app development agency with a number of hugely successful apps, most of which I had on my phone. I read an article that described him as a kind of wunderkind, an innovator who spent more time doing extreme sports than sitting in an office chair. He was divorced, a single dad with a young daughter and a reputation as a bit of a daredevil. What kind of a man went off skydiving when he had a child to look after? There was not a lot of information about the ex-wife, but it seemed she lived in Los Angeles. Lifestyles of the rich and famous, I thought with a disgusted snort.

Tate Sagarro's world couldn't have been further removed from my own. I'd been raised to value family, to love and appreciate my siblings and parents. I was not a thrill seeker at all, I hated going out even on the flattest of water on my father's boat. My pulse was sent racing by a sale at the local store and that was enough of an adrenaline rush for me.

My job interview took place online, in our kitchen at home. HumanITy's Head of HR interviewed me. An older lady with loads of make-up asked me a few questions, seemed bored by my responses and I did not expect to hear from the company again.

But then I did.

I had to travel to San Francisco for the second interview. I got a proper outfit for this meeting, borrowed money to fix my hair and actually put on some make up. The mascara made my eyes itchy and I had to stop myself from rubbing my eyes constantly. I knew I came across as nervous and twitchy, hardly the look you want to project when you're going after a job in Silicon Valley. By this time, I knew I wanted the job, if only because I would be able to work in Palo Alto. Something about the sun and the beach had changed my attitude. I liked the idea of getting ice cream after work, dipping my toes in the ocean.

Then, they kept me waiting for over an hour.

Finally, the head of HR called me in and informed me, very matter-of-factly, that I had gotten the job.

I couldn't believe it. I hadn't even met the CEO yet.

"He saw the recorded interview," said Jill Shapiro, the head of HR.

"He did?"

"He picked you," she said and got up. I had barely sat down.

"Can you start Monday, eight o'clock?"

Sure thing.

Except, nothing was sure about that job, from the word go.

Like, on Monday morning, when I reported for work and Mr. Sagarro didn't show. After a few hours, when I'd mastered the computer and the daily diary, which really wasn't that difficult, he still wasn't in the office. I phoned Jill and she told me in a very exasperated tone of voice, to get hold of him.

"This is your job now. He has Tamara at three. It's important, you tell him that. Find him," she said curtly.

"How?" I asked, realizing too late that she had already hung up the phone. I basically walked through the building, asking everyone I could find where I might get hold of Mr. Sagarro. In the end, it was the security guard, Mitch, who took pity on me.

"He's probably out surfing," he told me. "Waves have been awesome this week."

"Where?" I asked and he told me the name of the boss's favorite beach.

"Take the company car," Mitch said. "Can you drive?"

It took me over half an hour to get out of the city, following the instructions on my GPS. Then I drove around looking for the Jeep Mitch had mentioned, no mean feat, considering there were multiple access points to various beaches but finally, I found it.

Then, there was nothing else to do, but wait.

About an hour later, I saw a tall man coming across the sand and heading for the Jeep. He was wearing a wet suit, rolled halfway down his body, a surfboard tucked under his arm. His chest was strong, muscular, covered with thick blond hair. I got out of the car, went up to him.

"Mr. Sagarro?"

His eyes narrowed as he turned to face me, looking down at my shoes, high heels, which were sinking into the sand.

"Who're you?" he asked, his voice deep and melodic.

"Your new PA? Evie Gerick?" I stuck out my hand and he didn't even glance at it. Instead he opened his car door, reached for a towel and started drying himself off.

"Miss Shapiro asked me to find you, you have an urgent meeting at three?"

"She's married. Not a miss," he growled.

Then he drank some water and started to take off his wet suit, then whipping off his board shorts underneath.

I didn't know where to look.

The man was naked!

Completely naked!

"Who am I supposed to see at three?" He asked, turning to face me. I was so flustered that I took a step back and lost my footing in the sand.

Bloody high heel shoes! So much for being professional on my first day! How was I supposed to know I'd be running around in beach sand?! He leaned forward to grab my arm and pull me up.

"Steady on, there," he said, and I was vaguely aware of his groin area coming dangerously closer towards me. I blinked furiously, so mortified I could have died.

He was laughing! The bastard was grinning from ear to ear, as if he was really enjoying making me uncomfortable. I could feel my face reddening.

"Here, hold this," he said, handing me his towel as he reached for his clothes inside the car.

"So, the three o'clock?" he asked again, pulling on a pair of jeans.

"Uhm...yes...Tamara?"

"Who?"

I knew he was having me on by now.

I gave a deep sigh. "I don't know, that was the message and I gave it. It's my first day, I think I deserve a medal just for finding you at all."

He looked at me, his dark blue eyes twinkling mischievously.

"I think you're right," he said, a lopsided grin on his face.

"I'm awarding you the PA medal for Bravery and Courage Under Fire," he said and pretended to pin something onto my shirt. I'd taken off my jacket and I could feel his hand brush over my breast, the palm of his hand roughly grazing my nipple. He held my gaze the whole time and I didn't move, I barely breathed.

I could feel my nipple hardening under his touch.

"Thank you," I said, as primly as possible and stepped away.

He put on a white T-shirt and smiled at me.

"Meet me at the house tomorrow morning at seven," he said, getting into the car. "Ask Jill to send you the address."

With spinning tires, he drove off, leaving me behind.

My right breast was tingling where he had accidentally touched it.

It was accidental, wasn't it?

Suddenly, I couldn't be certain at all.

Chapter 2

T ate
After the morning meeting, I headed towards the elevator, keen to get out of the building as quickly as possible.

Before the door could close, Jill, the head of HR, pushed her way in.

"So glad I caught you!" she said, smiling at me.

This was a little game we played, one where she pretended not to have been looking for me for a while, sending messages and making calls that I didn't answer. My part was to pretend to be so busy that I missed all the important people looking for me, like her. Neither of us would ever admit to the truth; which was that I didn't like talking to people like her and tended to avoid them.

"Jill, what's up?"

"I wanted to remind you of the new PA starting on Monday."

I groaned out loud. "As long as she isn't as useless as that last one."

She gave me a look. "Petra was not useless."

I chuckled, "Please, that girl was a nervous wreck!"

"She almost lodged a complaint against you for sexual harassment!"

"Give me a break, as if that would've gone anywhere!"

We were on the ground floor now and I walked out with big strides, making it purposefully harder for Jill keep up with her tight skirt and rather stout frame.

"You did tell her to grow a pair! That could be construed as offensive and inappropriate language!"

"Come on!" I stopped walking and turned to face her.

Jill exhaled slowly. "You know we are busy talking to some big production companies. They are very sensitive to any kind of gender harassment stuff, any whiff of inappropriate behavior and they pull out of the deal!"

I sometimes regretted merging my company with Jill's organization. The new entity had made me millions, growing the company exponentially but it came with plenty of strings attached. Sometimes I felt like a dog on a leash, being yanked back by my master. Occasionally, it made me want to bite those in charge, other times I wanted to take a shit on their carpet, maybe chew up their metaphoric slippers.

"You picked this one, Evie Gerick," Jill reminded me. "I preferred the look of the other one, the graduate from Stanford."

"The statistics major? Wouldn't have lasted the day."

I had flipped through the photographs of all the applicants and something about Evie had caught my eye. She was pretty, which was important, obviously, but I wouldn't have admitted that to Jill. She certainly did not look fragile like Pathetic Petra, who had freaked out when I asked her to fire my personal trainer, saying she couldn't "crush someone's soul" like that. This had prompted me telling her to grow some balls, to which she had taken inter-galactic offence.

Something about Evie told me that she could take a bit of heat. Maybe it was the fact that she had two brothers, paid for her studies herself, worked part-time in a restaurant kitchen as a student. Those were high pressure environments, with very sharp knives and boiling water. I figured that she had enough balls for both of us. But I would definitely test her on that.

I had every intention of dropping her in the deep end on the first day.

She surprised me, finding me at the beach the way she had. It showed she had resources, a bit of fire, which I liked. What I didn't like, was the irritation she showed at having to use a few brain cells. It seemed she had a cushy job in mind when she started working for me.

After the afternoon at the beach, I made her come in early the next morning, then ensured I was out running, giving her time to meet my daughter, Summer, who was the best judge of character I knew. Summer was ten-going-on-thirty, she could see through the bullshit better than anyone, after all, her mother worked in the film industry in LA and Summer had more experience than most at trying to distinguish fairy glitter from facts.

I told Summer to let Evie in and told her she was my new PA, but nothing else.

Summer had been the first to call my previous PA Pathetic Petra, a name that had unfortunately stuck, and seemed very apt in retrospect. I was looking forward to hearing her opinion on Evie. If she hated her, Evie would be out the door faster than the personal trainer who'd tried to teach me to breathe.

When I got back from my run, Evie and Summer were in the kitchen, getting ready for school. Summer's nanny would pick up her up soon, but I liked that Evie had made Summer a lunch box and had even managed to do her hair. Summer was not the easiest kid in the world, with a father like me, who could blame her? I did take some pride in the fact that she was tough and a tomboy, totally hating anything pink or girly with a passion that disturbed some people.

I overheard part of their conversation.

"My dad took me skydiving once," said Summer. Little liar, as if I'd do that.

"Oh, yeah?" Evie said, "Did you like it?"

"It was okay," my little lying daughter said matter-of-factly.

"My dad took me ice skating on the lake when I was six years old and I fell through the ice," Evie said. "It took him a while to find me, I got pulled into the water."

"Were you scared?"

"Not so much scared as very, very cold. I hate being cold."

"Well, it doesn't get too cold around her," Summer said and I could tell by her voice that she approved of Evie.

"Glad to hear it," Evie said.

"You guys getting acquainted?" I asked, coming into the kitchen. Evie was dressed more casually today, in jeans and boots.

"So, what do you think," I asked Summer. "Will this one stick around?"

Summer shrugged non-committedly, pulling her backpack on and going out to meet her nanny for school.

"Thank you very much!" Evie called out after her and laughed a bit self-consciously.

"I tend to be hard on PAs," I said, watching her carefully.

"You don't say," she deadpanned.

"I'm going to make us some kale smoothies," I said, ignoring her. "Run me through my day."

Then I proceeded to put the blender on at high speed so I couldn't hear a word of what she said. When I stopped blending and she started talking again, I quickly switched it on again.

"I'm not a fan of the then-this, then-that," I said. "Just give me the most important parts."

"I don't know which meetings are the most important," she said.

I lifted an eyebrow, "I guess you'll have to figure it out fast, then," I said. I poured a few glasses and put them in front of her.

"Taste these and tell me which ones you like best."

She looked at the glasses of green liquid.

"I'm not... really... I mean..."

"You don't like kale?" I asked.

"Uhm, no, not really?"

"So what do you usually have for breakfast?"

"Coffee?"

"You need caffeine to get you going, you've got a problem right there. Wouldn't you prefer some natural energy fueling your body?"

When she didn't answer, I shoved the glasses towards her. "Tell me which one you prefer."

They were all the same, but I didn't want her knowing that.

She tasted them all, kept her face neutral and pointed to one, "That one. Now, I think you should get ready to take your nine o'clock call. I think that one is important."

"You think?"

She seemed to stumble over her words. "Well, I don't know... The sender is Rachel Levy. But there is a report attached and she says in the mail that she wants to discuss..."

"Did you read the report?"

She shook her head.

"Read it quickly and give me the gist of it."

She stared at me like she didn't know what to do.

"Now!"

I fetched my laptop and shoved it towards her, letting her open the mail and scan the document. I watched her pull herself together, get over her annoyance with me, deciding to get the job done. I had already read the report, already knew that I didn't need to meet with Rachel.

"The report seems to focus on staff compliance and an evaluation of initial feedback..."

I interrupted her, "The gist, Evie, what is bottom line here?" I didn't have to fake my impatience. I needed someone who could get to the point quickly. This was a crucial part of her job, reading through the blah-blah and finding the bombshells.

"They're happy," Evie said curtly. "The bottom line is; staff have adjusted and things are satisfactory."

"Great," I responded with equal curtness. "Send her an email thanking her for the report and ask if she wishes to discuss anything else in greater detail, and if so, why."

Evie bit her lip.

"Okay," she nodded.

"That's it for today," I said, turning away.

"You're... not coming into the office?" she asked, uncertainty in her voice.

"I'll be working," I said, turning back to face her, poker-faced.

"You just... won't be there physically?" she guessed.

"Bingo!" I tapped a finger in her direction. "Now you've got it! Read as many emails as possible, figure out what is important and what isn't. Let me know about the rest of the day too."

"Where will you be?" she asked me.

I rolled my eyes. This was like talking to my ex-wife, whom I had gotten rid of, very successfully.

"I'll answer my phone if you call. Don't send more than five texts," I warned her, then waved my hand at her. Dismissed. She slunk out of the house and I thought to myself that the jury was still out on this one.

But by dinnertime, me and Summer having sushi outside on the patio, I still hadn't fired her. Somehow, I'd gotten into a tech review by a developer friend of mine and that had sidetracked me.

"Is Evie still around?" Summer asked me. She was dressed in an oversized hoodie with huge sneakers, looking like a kid-sized gangster-rapper, which was her preferred look at the moment.

"No..." I said.

"But she is still working for you?"

I shrugged. "I guess..."

"I like her," Summer said and took a bite out of her nigiri.

"You do?" I was surprised. Summer liked almost nobody. Most days, I didn't think she particularly liked me and I was her father.

Summer nodded. "She's real."

Maybe I'd give Evie another day, I thought.

Chapter 3

E vie
     My mother calls after a few days to hear how it's going in the new job.

"Fine," I say.

"It's going well?" She asks again. Clearly, I haven't convinced her.

"Oh, yeah. I'm busy but I'm loving it," I say, working up as much enthusiasm as I possibly can.

I don't know why I'm lying to my mother, possibly to avoid admitting that I can't even do something as basic as being someone's personal assistant.

The truth is, I have no idea what I'm doing.

I get up early to go through Tate's emails, then try to figure out who is important and who isn't, how to read his messages and prioritize the ones he'd want to deal with. I've come to realize that he basically wants to speak to no-one and that I am supposed to block most people wanting access to him, feeding them a rich diet of lies that sound completely different to whatever they heard last time. I've come to learn that he is a genius who can't work in the office, must be left to his own devices to go rock climbing or play golf where he, only occasionally, mind you, gets fantastic ideas, which he then feeds to his team of fabulous developers who then make everything happen in the dark like clever little elves.

This I learned from Summer, his daughter and the best source of information on all things Tate.

I have to fetch her from school one day when Summer's nanny calls in sick. I find the school, then wait outside for the girl to jump in. I drive her home after buying her a MacDonalds burger for lunch.

"My father would fire you if he knew you gave me this for lunch," Summer remarks, looking at me cannily.

I shrug. "I wasn't hired as your cook."

The fridge is filled with all kinds of readymade meals with labels like quinoa and lentils or brown rice pilaf. Apparently there is an executive chef who comes in every morning to cook and leave for the day. Summer was supposed to eat some pumpkin green curry today.

She grins at me. "I won't tell if you won't," she says, tucking into the burger with gusto.

"Deal!"

Later, after I've finished helping her with her homework, she asks me how it is going working for her father.

"Not well," I admit. "I don't think he likes me a lot." Confiding in a child is a new low for me. But it turns out to be the best thing I could have done.

"Dad hates being a boss," she tells me. "He wants to be creative. But he needs space to do that, for his thoughts to fly." She makes hand movements to indicate birds flying.

"Really?"

"How do you think he came up with Calmia?" she asks me. The app, a best-selling mental health program, became a bestseller a few years ago. I have used it myself, although not since coming to work for Tate Sagarro. Now it seems a bit close to home, somehow.

He was cave diving," Summer tells me. "He got this idea of people being underwater, surrounded by calm and tranquility, cutting out all noise, all sound."

"Then he got other people to build it?" I ask.

She nods. "That's what he loves to do, think up ideas. Not sit at a desk and answer phones. That's what he has you for."

This is how the penny drops. Because by now I know that I desperately want this job to work out. I don't really know why, except that Tate is like no one I have ever met. He is simultaneously wonderful and terrible, arrogant and funny, incredibly smart but terribly obtuse about some things.

Thanks to Summer, I know to cut his diary down to two calls a day, maximum.

I filter all his messages out. In the mornings, I wait for him before he goes running, firing words at him like balls from a tennis machine.

"Wallace DeBryan?" I might say.

"Yeah?" He could reply if mildly interested.

"You want to do a ten minute catch-up call?"

"No."

That will be it. No call.

I still get it wrong, but two weeks later, I've still got a job and I start to think that maybe, just maybe, I'll get the hang of this after all. It is exhilarating to be a part of this process, of facilitating genius. Maybe a small part of it is attraction too, but I can't admit to any of this.

Not yet.

Tate is my boss and I can't let feelings get in the way of the process.

At least, this is what I tell myself.

Until the night of the Kigana presentation.

Kigana Play is a Japanese game company that has come to the US and has been trying to get a meeting with Tate for weeks. I put them off by letting them meet with one of Tate's most trusted developers, a guy called Haroon, whom he trusts implicitly when it comes to tech development. A meeting was set up for the Kigana delegation and I was asked to draft some brochures and come up with a presentation. The meeting was set up for early the next morning.

Then, as I'm putting finishing touches on the brochures, which I have just spent hours getting right, Tate calls me and tells me the meeting is off.

"What?"

"I am heading off to Iceland tomorrow," he says. "Arctic swim."

"You're kidding."

"Nope, weather's great, it's finally clearing and conditions are right for it. I'm leaving in the morning."

"But Kigana..."

"You do it," he says. "Haroon knows the whole deal by now and you can make a call on it."

"What do you mean?" I ask quickly. "I thought you were positive about it?"

"I was going to wait for the pitch," he says.

"I don't know much about educational apps," I say, anxiety building.

"Neither do I," says Tate. "I usually go on my gut feel."

"My gut is up to shit," I say.

Tate laughs. "But what does your shitty gut tell you on this one?"

"I don't know," I say, exasperated.

"Figure it out, it's your call," he says and the line goes dead.

I stare at the phone for a long, long time.

This is insane, I think. How can he possibly entrust me with this kind of responsibility after two weeks on the job?!

But I go out, get myself some takeaway coffee and then I come back and I work solidly for the rest of the evening. I call Haroon and tell him to give me his elevator pitch for the app.

"Why?" he asks annoyed. "Isn't Tate going to be there?" I can tell he's invested in the idea moving forward by now.

"No," I tell him honestly. "He's going somewhere. You have to convince me."

There is a pause on the line. Then I hear him muttering, "Fuck this."

"I know," I sigh. "But this is how it is."

So, Haroon goes for it, giving it his best shot. Then I spend the rest of the evening trying to figure out how original the idea is and if it will work.

I nearly get the fright of my life when at round eleven o'clock, I suddenly hear a voice say near my ear, "What's the verdict?"

It's Tate.

I hadn't heard him come in, so engrossed had I been in the work.

"Jesus! You scared me!"

He smiles. "Sorry," not sounding sorry at all.

I take a deep sigh and shake my head.

"I don't know, it doesn't really work for me," I admit. "I hate to be the one who pulls the plug, though."

"It's not you," he says. "It's me. I'll pull the plug."

"But they will know it's me who made you do it."

He lifts an eyebrow. "Made me do it? You think anyone can make me do anything I don't want to?"

I smile and shake my head.

I switch my computer off, take my bag and walk to the elevator with him, turning off the lights as I do. I'm the last one on my floor and by the time I reach the elevator, the floor is dark and we can barely see the elevator.

"I like the dark, don't you?" he says in a husky voice, close to my ear.

"Depends," I manage to say.

"On what?" he asks.

I know everything is word play with Tate and I'm still thinking up the kind of response I think he'll want to hear when his mouth is on mine and he is pushing me against the wall, his body rock hard against mine.

I don't say anything, but I kiss him back, matching his intensity, surprising myself with my response. I hadn't realized I felt this way about him, but suddenly, it's obvious to me. The way I've been working like a maniac to figure him out, to get into his mind. Our bodies intertwine, my leg twists around his, pulling him closer. He is strong, when he puts his arms around me, it feels like he is going to crush me and I find myself incredibly turned on by him. He moves his hands under my top and he's kissing me roughly. I can feel myself getting wet and excited as I shrug off my jeans right there in front of the elevator, in the dark lobby of the office building. When he enters me, I feel a jolt of electricity course through my body, energy pulsing through every cell in my body. I wrap my legs around him and he thrusts into me, banging my back against the wall. It's rough and it's exciting and before I know it, it's over.

I am too stunned to realize what has happened.

Chapter 4

Tate

The next morning, when Summer comes down for breakfast, she stops in her tracks.

"I thought you were gone already," she says.

"Change of plan," I say.

She stares at me.

"Why?"

I couldn't exactly tell her how I'd woken up two hours ago, in the dark, and lay in bed thinking that the last thing that I felt like doing was to plunge myself into freezing water in the coldest place on earth. I'd just had another kind of shock to the system, and I wanted to deal with that first.

"I changed my mind," I said.

She looked at me for a moment or two, a direct and unflinching stare that she must have inherited from me. My ex-wife, Star, wasn't one for confrontation, but Summer did not like to shy away from the truth, no matter how uncomfortable it was.

"Why?" she asked again

I shrugged. I'd learnt it was better not to lie to her.

As I expected, she accepted my evasive answer and settled for her breakfast of toast.

"I could make you a smoothie?" I offered and she pulled a face.

"Yuck, I'd rather go hungry."

I smiled at that.

"Star called last night," she said between mouthfuls of cereal.

"Oh?"

Since an early age, Summer had called her mother by her first name. Even though Star denied it, I had a feeling that she had requested this, to make her seem more free and unencumbered.

Summer pulled a face. "I think she is getting serious with that Trevor guy."

"What gave you that idea?" I asked.

My ex-wife had hooked up with a film studio executive a few months ago and this time, it seemed to last.

"She asked me if I liked him," Summer said, an expression of intense dislike on her face. "I said no and she asked if I could try."

"Well, you could try," I said, trying to hide the amusement I felt at the thought of Summer having to try to like someone.

"I could pretend," Summer amended, looking at me. "I think that is what she wants," she said with a sigh. "She said something about us coming out there to spend time with her, Trevor and his son."

"Us?" I asked. This was news to me. Did Star want me to come out to LA too?

"Yes, you too," Summer grinned, enjoying pulling me into the drama.

This was the first time I'd heard of it. "She said she'd talk to you," Summer added.

This meant Summer was probably right, Star could be thinking about taking things to the next level with this Trevor.

"We'll see," I said. I had no intention of going to see Star and her new lover in their love nest up in La-la-land. If she wanted to see us, she could come here, which I knew would not happen. Star liked to pretend that she had never lived here, had never been something as boring as a wife and mother with a house and dinner to cook for her family. She had recreated her image as a stylist to the stars. Someone glamorous and above the drudgery of normal life.

I decided to immerse myself in work.

But my thoughts kept straying to the night before and to Evie. It shouldn't really have surprised me that it happened, and yet it did. Over the past two weeks, things had changed between us. From a rather rocky start, she had managed to find her feet quickly. In a matter of days, she had figured out exactly what I wanted. She developed an attitude with people from work, and it was amusing to see how she dealt even with important people. Like, when Max Topper, the CEO of a major tech company called to talk to me, and she told him I was not available.

I was standing at her desk, talking to her about some meeting I had to attend in Washington the following week when the phone rang.

"I'm sorry, Mr. Topper," Evie said in a crisp, professional voice. "Mr. Sagarro is out all afternoon in a development meeting. If you leave a detailed messaged, I will make sure he gets it."

"That was impressive!" I said after the call.

She blushed, which was cute.

Then she confessed that Summer had shared some tips with her on how to deal with me.

"The rat!" I said. "How did you manage to get that kind of highly-confidential info out of her? Waterboarding? Sleep deprivation?"

She looked sheepish. "Actually, I fed her MacDonalds."

She knew how I felt about nutrition and healthy food, but she'd been helping me out with Summer because the nanny was sick. I kind of admired the underhanded way she had gone about getting in Summer's good books. It was the sort of thing I would have done myself. Looking at the outcome, what was one high calorie, super processed and preservative-laden meal compared with an extremely productive employee who was able to truly assist me in my work?

I started noticing other things about her as well.

She was attractive but not drop-dead gorgeous. Somehow, I liked that. She was natural, real. She didn't wear fake eyelashes or acrylic nails, didn't have loads of make up on her face. Some days she had her hair in a messy ponytail, or in a bun with a pencil. That made me think of a scatterbrained librarian and all kinds of fantasies popped into my head about taking the pencil out and watching her hair fall on her shoulders.

I'd never had fantasies about my personal assistants before. I'd never been romantically involved with anyone at work, it had never occurred to me to view my female colleagues and employees as anything other than professionals working with me.

But it was different with Evie.

As the days passed, I started wondering about her, who she was in her private life, what she liked doing. Did she exercise? Do sports? Did she watch a lot of TV? I sometimes asked questions but she tended to be vague when it came to herself. Instead of discouraging me, that only seemed to heighten my interest in her.

I started watching her.

When she took calls that seemed personal, I would try to get into the vicinity to hear what she was saying. When she was at home, talking to Summer, I would listen to their conversations, but never learned much. It was infuriating. I was used to women who loved talking about themselves, what they liked and didn't like, but Evie was not like this. One morning I overheard her asking Summer where we went for ice-cream.

"Are you kidding?" Summer exploded with mock outrage. "All that sugar, dairy?! We don't poison our bodies like that!"

"Right," Evie said and they laughed, ganging up against me.

Then Summer said, "But there is a place in town that Dad once took me to, it's sugar-free, dairy-free, everything free."

"Sounds delicious," Evie said in a sarcastic voice.

"Totally," Summer responded.

I was glad they were bonding, of course, but not at my expense.

Still, I now knew Evie liked ice cream. She was clearly not health conscious, but then at her age, was I?

I didn't want to think of myself at her age, when all I could think about was work and making it in this highly-competitive environment. John and I had just gotten our first app out, a program for high school kids, based on the idea of online dating. But the functionality was limited to only positive responses; they could like, love or find each other funny. The kids, of course, still found a way to exploit it, but at many schools, the app was used the way it was intended to, as a fun way for kids to interact and get to know each other, a safe space to share videos and build confidence and a sense of community. LikeMe became huge and before we knew it, we were no longer working on a fun project for computer science class, but developing a viable platform that could make us millions. Both of us dropped out of college to focus on the project, to the dismay of our parents.

But those were the days when we lived off sugar and caffeine, burning calories faster than we could ingest them. We didn't worry about our bodies, brain fog or energy levels dropping due to lack of sleep. Our twenty-year-old bodies were designed to be pushed and we pushed them.

My attraction to Evie grew and even though I was aware of it, I thought I had it under control. Until the night I decided to pop into the office and see if she was still there, working away on the mad assignment I'd given her. I had already decided against the project, there was a flood of similar stuff on the market and it wasn't innovative enough for us. But I wanted to see if Evie would arrive at the same conclusion, and how she'd go about it.

When she was there, sitting alone in the office, her legs pulled up in the office chair, shoes kicked off, it did something to me.

I should have turned around, gone home.

But I didn't.

And then, in the dark, it was too easy. She was walking ahead of me, I caught the smell of her hair. A clean shampoo smell, no perfume, nothing messing with the wonderful scent of her and desire overcame me. Simple as that.

But it couldn't happen again.

It wouldn't.

As far as I was concerned, it had not happened at all.

If she could live with that, good.

If she couldn't, I would have no problem finding someone else to do her job.

Chapter 5

Evie

I almost didn't go in to work the next day.

How was I going to face him after what had happened?

I couldn't look at myself in the mirror, how could I begin to deal with what I had done? Sleeping with my boss? That was not me at all! No matter how many excuses I could come up with (and I could come up with many), I knew I should have known better.

I would've quit and gone back home, the only problem was, that would mean quitting and going back home. I didn't want to go home and I didn't want to resign from my job. I liked working in the city, being surrounded by the buzz of all that creative energy. Nobody would have thought anything of it back home if I told them it didn't work out. They would accept it without question, but then what would I do? I would be the baby of the family again, never taken seriously by anyone.

Here, I was someone.

I was the way to get to Tate Sagarro, one of the brilliant brains of the tech industry. People watched me as I came in to work in the morning, eagerly waiting for a second of my time, trying to go up the stairs with me, bribing me with coffee to get five minutes with Tate. I had found my feet over the past few weeks, getting into a groove at work. I didn't want to give that up because of one mistake.

Because that is what it was.

I was sure he felt the same way. Afterwards, when we had taken the elevator down, we had barely talked or looked at each other. He'd offered to take me home and I'd quickly said something about already having a ride, which we both knew was not true, but he seemed grateful to accept.

I remembered that he was away on his trip, which meant I wouldn't see him at work, giving me some time to think up a strategy. I went for coffee as soon as I got into the office. As I was stirring extra sugar into my cup, someone tapped me on the shoulder.

It was Haroon.

"So?" he asked, impatiently bouncing on his feet. "Are we a go for this morning?"

"What do you mean? I told you last night, the Kigana meeting is off?"

I had told him that, hadn't I? I had forgotten all about the meeting with the Japanese game manufacturer.

"Yes, but Tate said he'd think about it. Told me to give him a few hours to look at my proposal."

"When was this?"

"About ten o'clock last night?"

That must have been before he came in to the office, to see me. Before everything happened.

"You haven't spoken to him since?"

He shook his head. Haroon looked stressed and somewhat disheveled, like he had worked through the night.

"The last time I spoke to him, last night, he said he'd decided against it," I said gently.

"But why?" Haroon's voice filled with agony. I couldn't think why he was so personally and emotionally involved in the app.

"He's gone off education," I said, making it up as I went along. I had to come up with something, though, I could see Haroon needed an explanation. "He says the market is saturated."

I left Haroon in the cafeteria, nodding to himself and muttering furiously. If I had seen him on the street, I would have thought he was mentally unwell, someone suffering from a condition. But at HumanITy, he fit right in.

I went up to my desk, tried to focus on work, going through Tate's emails as usual.

My phone pinged.

A message from Tate.

My heart started beating faster. Was this it? Was he going to fire me?

The message was curt, to the point:

Have decided against trip. Will be working from home. Am available on phone.

I read the message a few times. It was short, professional and direct. He was communicating about work and work only. I felt a huge sense of relief, a great weight lifting from my chest as I sat back in my chair and exhaled deeply.

We would carry on as if nothing had happened. Last night, having sex in the office, never happened. When I went out for lunch, I carefully looked around, checked the cameras on the floor and saw that they were angled away from the elevator lobby. The elevator doors would be visible, but we had been in the corner, against the wall. I couldn't look in that direction, but my mind went there anyway, the way I had gripped his back with my legs, pushing him deeper into me, the smell of salt and soap as he buried his face in my neck.

No.

I couldn't allow myself to go there.

I had to stop my thoughts from lingering on the way he had looked at me and kissed me. It was a moment of madness and it was over now. I could focus on work again.

There couldn't be anything more between us, obviously. We were too different, on completely separate walks of life. He was older, he had a child, a company and to him, the world was a juicy buffet from which he could pick whatever he wanted to eat. It wasn't the same for me. I was young and inexperienced, trying everything for the first time, making mistakes, learning. I wasn't fearless like him, I didn't like challenges and problems, didn't enjoy finding answers to complex riddles. I certainly didn't like the idea of jumping from planes or plunging down gorges suspended by a thin piece of rope.

Life had been enough of an adventure for me so far.

Tate wasn't scared of anything, and while I wouldn't say I was scared of everything, there were a lot of things that made me nervous. Flying, for instance, was not something I was fond of. I didn't like boats or motorcycles, I was not sporty at all. Reaching for a remote control was my idea of exercise.

I went down for lunch and saw some girls walking past me and looking at me strangely. I went to the bathroom to check and saw, much to my horror, that I had put on my top the wrong way around. I was wearing the back to front and the front to back. This is what happened when you didn't look in the mirror in the morning! I quickly changed my top and put on some make up, fixing my hair as well.

Why hadn't Haroon said something this morning?

Was it possible he hadn't noticed that my T-shirt was looking all wrong, choking my neck in front, while hanging all baggy at the back?

More weird, was that I hadn't noticed it myself, so obsessed had I been with what had happened the night before.

I took a few deep breaths, calmed myself down.

This was going to be okay, I told myself.

We had done something silly, it didn't mean anything. Tate probably slept with all of his PAs. It wasn't a thought I particularly liked, but it helped kill any feelings that might have been trying to take root. He was the kind of guy who liked women, obviously, but he didn't seem to do relationships or anything serious.

A few days passed, then one afternoon, a lawyer from the third floor had come up, asking to see him. She was beautiful, the kind of woman I could see him with. Groomed, high heels, skinny like a model. I had felt her eyes rake me over before asking if Tate was in. When I said he wasn't, she'd said in a deep, husky voice.

"Tell him, it's Jacqueline."

I had to say, again, that he really wasn't in. I wasn't using code for keeping out people he didn't want to see. He was actually out of the office.

She pouted, for real. Her lips kind of pushed out while she folded her arms.

"He hasn't called me," she said, sulkily.

It was kind of funny. She clearly had no problem letting me know that they had something personal going on and that she was feeling slighted by him.

"Should I give him a message?" I asked.

"Like what?" she asked me.

I was speechless for a moment. She wanted me to come up with a message? How was I supposed to know what she wanted to say? On the other hand, it was pretty obvious. She wanted to see him.

"I'll tell him to call you," I said.

She thought about it. "No," she said, shaking her head. "Don't do that."

Then she turned around and walked out, without saying anything else. When I mentioned to Tate later that she had been in the office, he had asked what she wanted, like she was just another colleague he worked with. I said I didn't know and waited for his response. But he shrugged it off and asked if there were any other messages. Whatever he meant to her, she clearly did not have the same effect on him.

Me, on the other hand, I liked relationships, proper ones.

I didn't do flings or one-night-stands.

This was the first time, ever.

And the last.

Definitely.

Chapter 6

Tate

When I arrive at home, Summer is outside with the nanny, having just returned from the shops.

Both of them turn to look at me, the nanny's mouth opening.

I get a kick out of that.

Summer frowns, of course, and shakes her head.

I pull into the driveway, revving the car a bit for effect.

"Do you really need a new car?" Summer asks me, sarcastically.

Of course I didn't need a new car.

But I wanted it.

"Definitely," I said, my face all serious as Summer rolled her eyes and went into the house.

I'd be selling the Porsche. I made a mental note to send Evie a message to contact the dealer I worked with to go about selling the car. I'd had it a few months, longer than usual actually. I never held on to cars too much.

Cars and women, I tended to have a similar approach to. I liked the feeling of a new car, sitting in the clean seats, pushing the limits. The same with women, I suppose. At first, getting to know someone new, hearing their stories for the first time, enjoying that buzz that never seems to last past a few weeks. I couldn't stand the way a relationship seemed to sag and lose shape after a few months, when the bitchy comments and the demands started coming in, tempers fraying when I didn't call according to their schedule.

After the divorce, I resolved not to get married again. Short-term relationships were best. I didn't hold on to them for too long, both cars and women. It sounded ruthless, I guess, but it worked.

I'd never slept with a PA before, though.

That was a first.

I'd never even been attracted to one of them before, and some of them were real lookers. There was that one girl, a part-time model for Victoria Secret, as she proudly stated on her CV. But I'd never even looked at her twice, even when she'd openly flirted with me, one night at some event, she'd slid her hand up my thigh and grabbed my cock.

I'd leant over to whisper something into her ear, she'd smiled at me, and then I told her she was fired. Pleasure and work did not mix.

Yet, somehow, with Evie, it had.

We'd managed to avoid the topic for about a week after we'd had sex. Then, one day she'd come to the house to talk about a meeting and we'd simply pretended that nothing had happened. She seemed as keen as me to move on. I felt it needed to be addressed though, I didn't want it hanging over me.

"The other night..." I started.

"Nothing happened," she quickly said, looking me in the eye. "It looked like it could, there was something there, but then we came to our senses and nothing happened."

She sounded so sure of herself, it was almost like she believed it.

"Okay," I said, but I wasn't convinced.

"Because we're friends, right? And you're my boss. And something like that just wouldn't be right?"

I had to admire the way she handled it. No awkwardness, all straight-forward and businesslike.

"Sure, we're friends," I said.

"Excellent," she said and there was a quick smile, which made me see how nervous she was.

"Now, unless you need me for anything else, I'm going to be off."

"Wait," I said, keeping my face straight. "I need you..."

There was a look of sheer terror on her face. Then I winked at her and saw her blush. Ah, it was too easy, I thought.

"I need you to pick up my dry cleaning in the city and bring the suits back here. I want to wear the suit to dinner tonight."

"Right," she said. "Restaurant is booked, Miss Cousins has confirmed."

I looked closely at her face but there was nothing there. If she seemed uncomfortable about my date with Jacqueline, she didn't show it. This was good, we could move on. Perhaps the little fuck in the office could stay just that.

It was a pity though, because I'd liked it.

It had been fun.

Quick, exciting and quite a thrill to do it right there in the elevator lobby. She'd responded to my touch, she'd been so ready, so incredibly wet. It made me hard just thinking about it. With other women, it was usually so complicated. Sex wasn't simple with them. They wanted a few dinners, a weekend away, some luxury place, then wining and dining. It was usually a game with several moves. I always played to win, of course. But with Evie there had been none of that.

She seemed conservative in some ways, even innocent, the way she buttoned her shirts up to the top, never wearing skirts over the knee. But she had no compunction taking them off though, the ease with which she'd slipped her top over her head, dropping it on the floor.

I didn't really want to see Jacqueline but I knew she'd been wanting to hook up.

I needed to get my head off Evie anyway.

Best way to do that was to find someone else.

I knew Jacqueline was keen. She was gorgeous too, everything I liked in a woman, smart and pretty, a good sense of humor. We drank wine, ate some food, finished it with dessert. I took her back to my place and watched her take off her clothes, doing a bit of striptease for me. She had a great body, lean and tight, not an ounce of fat on her. Her skin was tanned, even all over, she was perfect in every way.

When I kissed her in bed, she felt wrong somehow, though.

I found myself thinking of Evie, whose mouth had been so soft, the lips untouched by the plastic surgeon's needle.

My phone rang.

I pulled back. "Just a second," I said, filling my voice with regret.

I leaned over to answer my phone.

"Okay," I said. "So run it by me slowly again, when you entered the code, what popped up?" I got out of bed, walked over to the window, unbothered by the fact that I was naked. I looked out of the window, could see the waves breaking in the dark.

"Yes, okay, and then what?" I said, impatiently, as if I was talking to some developer in the middle of a crisis. In fact, the line was dead, I was talking to an empty line.

I had set up a call via an app I had, in case I'd wanted an out. It came in handy every now and then. If things worked out with Jacqueline, then I'd ignore it, but if I wanted an out, this was a convenient way to do that.

It was working.

Behind me, I could hear Jacqueline getting out of bed and putting on her clothes.

I turned around to look at her, miming my regret and putting my hands together as if begging her to forgive me.

"Yes, yes," I said, pretending to listen to someone on the line again.

She snuck out of the room as soon as she was dressed and I took a shower as soon as I saw her getting into a taxi and going home.

I turned on the hot water and closed my eyes, thought of Evie in her starched work shirts, her firm thighs and how she squeezed them around me. I grew hard very fast, gasping with pleasure as I fucked her again, in my mind, in the corner of the elevator lobby.

Afterwards, I send Jacqueline a message saying I was sorry about the evening, that we should reschedule.

Then, I thought of ways of seeing Evie again.

Once wasn't enough.

That much was clear.

I needed more.

I was sure Evie felt the same way.

She'd enjoyed it as much as I had, of that I was certain. The way she'd moved with me, moaned when I thrusted, there was a synchronicity to our movements that didn't happen often.

It didn't mean anything, of course.

It was just an itch that needed to be scratched, properly.

Then I'd be able to move on, as before.

I wondered how I would share this information with her, make a joke about it even, how we maybe didn't get it right the first time because I'm still thinking about it and would like to put an end to the whole thing? It could work, I thought.

Could have worked, I should say.

Because then Evie's boyfriend came and ruined everything. I didn't even know she was seeing anyone. But when I got to work the next day, there was a gigantic bouquet of roses, completely over the top, sitting on her desk. She'd gone out to get coffee for my meeting and I peered among the petals for a card. I found one, it only said: Thanks for a beautiful night x.

That little x, the kiss, gave it away.

I knew she was seeing someone last night. As she'd left my house, I heard her on the phone, her voice quite altered, not like when she talked to me at all. It was more relaxed, playful even. She said she was looking forward to seeing someone later and clearly, it had gone well.

I didn't like the stab of jealousy I felt. I was not a jealous guy. I took what I wanted and I moved on. This was an unexpected bump in the road. I intended getting rid of it like I got rid of everything that got in my way.

Chapter 7

E vie
       There was this huge bouquet of roses delivered to the office.

There was no name on it, just a message saying thank you for a beautiful night. I assumed they were from Jacqueline for Tate. Their date clearly had gone well. He was in a meeting with a developer and the shut door meant he was not to be disturbed. Then I got busy doing other things, he'd sent me out on errands to buy things, turned out Tate hated shopping. Something I really did not mind all that much.

By the time I got back, he had already left for the day.

On my desk were ten cardboard boxes.

I looked inside, and found they were protein-based shakes.

There was a post-it note, which said: Sample all and pick one.

I had to laugh.

This was typical Tate, making me choose something that was bound to be wrong. We had completely different taste buds and what tasted good to me would be awful for him. But he kept telling me he didn't have time to waste. I was to be his taster, as if we were on an ancient court, like in Egypt or Mesopotamia or something. If I dropped dead, well, that was another PA gone but in the bigger picture, who would really care?

I took the shakes to the cafeteria and proceeded to mix them all up, tasting them and scoring them from one to ten.

"What are you doing?" a young woman asked, coming in to get yoghurt from the fridge.

I explained my assignment.

She shook her head. "This is your job? Tasting protein shakes?"

I nodded and laughed. "This one is quite good, what do you think?"

She smiled and sipped. "I like that one, yeah! What is it made of?"

"This one is pea protein, I think."

The woman was called May, she said she was working in New Projects. She'd been there for six months but she was thinking of quitting. "I have no life," she said mournfully. "I'm always working and never seem to make any headway."

She was part of a team working on an app customizing dog voices. "It's not really what I saw myself doing as a kid," she said pulling a face.

"Do you think I thought I'd be doing this?!" I said pointing at the shakes.

We both laughed.

Despite how crazy it looked though, I liked what I did.

"There is method to his madness," I told May. "Tate Sagarro looks insane but he isn't. It took me a while to figure that out."

She looked at me. "Yeah?"

I couldn't tell her how we'd slept together and how awkward things had been for a while. But it seemed that he then hooked up with Jacqueline and even though it did bother me a bit, the thought that he had moved on so quickly. Somehow, I'd let myself think that what had happened between us had been special. How naïve could a girl be?! I shook myself out of that dream. A man like Tate deserved a woman who was experienced and knew something about the world. I'd looked Jacqueline up on the internet, saw that she had studied business in France and worked in Barcelona when she was young. Her profile said she was unmarried and I did a little digging, finding out she was divorced. Like Tate. They had a lot in common. More than we did, I had to admit.

I focused on work, and tried to make friends with my room-mate Luisa, who was studying at the nearby University of San Francisco. She had a lively group of friends who went out almost every evening and I joined them as often as I could, to take my mind off Tate. Luisa didn't believe in having one boyfriend, going out with many male friends, flirting with all of them and leading them on. Some of them flirted with me to make her jealous and it was fun in a way. One of them, Xavier, had seemed to take an interest in me. I didn't feel the same about him, but as Luisa, pointed out, he didn't need to know that. I needed to get Tate out of my head. I seemed to be thinking about him. All the time. It was like when he'd touched me that night, he'd switched something on in me, awakened something. I couldn't help it. I'd spend all night with Luisa and Xavier, dancing and drinking and having a good time, but when I went to bed, all I could think about was Tate, his hands on me, the way he'd pushed me against the wall, hard enough to knock out my breath.

But I only told May about Tate, the innovator. I couldn't say anything about him, the man.

"The app you're working on now? Imagine being a kid in hospital, sick with cancer or something, missing your family back home. If you had an app where the dog barked just like your Fluffy did at home, or it squeaked like your pet hamster did?"

"Huh," May said, seemingly impressed. "I hadn't thought of it like that."

"I mean, can there be anything more rewarding and meaningful than cheering up a sick kid? Giving them a will to live?"

"You're good at this!" May said admiringly.

But I'd spent a whole day listening to Tate going on and on about this particular app. He'd taken his new car out for a drive and I remember being nervous about being out of the office. He'd insisted, though, taking me on long back country roads where he could really push the speed limit. I'd closed my eyes, convinced we were going to crash and die. He kept going on about the engine and the torque or something. I stopped listening and started praying, talking to God, to the universe, whoever was out there listening.

Finally, thank goodness, he stopped the car.

We got out, my legs shaking from that drive. I didn't trust myself to speak and for about five minutes, Tate didn't say a word. We were at the edge of a bluff, looking out at the sea. There were sea gulls flying and screeching overhead and the wind was cold. I hugged myself, wondering where I'd left my jacket. At the house? In the office?

But Tate was oblivious to all of this.

"Imagine you could upload your favorite sound on an avatar, and picture it whenever you needed to. Like this scene here, imagine we could capture it with audio and visual? Then, when you need to be calm, peaceful, you press a switch and presto, you are there."

But I wasn't feeling calm and peaceful. I was cold and uncomfortable. I wanted to get out of there, get a cup of coffee and something with sugar, carbohydrates.

Tate was in a completely different world, "The gear is important. Nothing clunky like a VR headset. More like glasses, with lenses that don't appear to change."

I was counting the seconds till we could leave. I didn't dare interrupt him. It was obvious to me that this was how the man worked, this was how he created and innovated. While the rest of us were in the real world, he was off in some weird space. Brought on by the speed of the car and being out of the office, the freedom of the road.

He told me to drive the car back while he made notes and recorded voice notes for the development team. I drove back much slower than he did but he didn't notice that either, completely focused on his thoughts and the execution of his idea. He had no idea if it would work, he told me later, but that would be up to the developers. People like May, it turned out.

"I don't think I'm genius material like him," she muttered as she helped me carry back the shake boxes up to the office. The winning product we kept separated and the others we packed on the ground.

"So this is where the magic happens," she said, looking over at Tate's office.

But this wasn't it at all. The magic happened in his head, at random intervals, when he was doing one thing and focusing on another. I had seen it happen. It was strange at first, but I was getting used to it now. I had never known anyone like him.

"Do you like Asian food?" May asked me suddenly. "My brother has opened a shop in front of our house." She rolled her eyes. "It's not great, but it is cheap."

"I love Asian food!" I said with a big smile. She invited me for dinner and after work, we met up and took an Uber back to her parents' small home in Chinatown. I had not been to this part of the city yet and was amazed at the hustle and bustle.

"My grandparents came to the US after the war," she said. "They couldn't speak any English and my father got a job sweeping floors in a restaurant. After a few years, he became a waiter, then finally, he took over the place. My father grew up here. He wanted my brother to become a doctor. Instead, what does he do?" she pulled up her shoulders. "He opened a restaurant!"

We laughed. Life was strange sometimes.

May's brother Eddie was taller than May, but he had the same quick smile and warm brown eyes. There was a little porch in front of their house, which he'd decorated with paper lanterns, giving it a festive feel. Plastic chairs were placed next to each other and most of the customers had to share tables but I liked the friendly atmosphere. It was a kind of pop-up shop and he brought two steaming bowls of rice with a wonderfully spicy sauce that seemed to set my entire mouth on fire.

"I should have warned you!" May laughed.

I shook my head, tears running down my cheeks as I tried to pretend I was fine.

"I thought you could take it!"

"I so can't! Seriously!"

Eddie brought me a milder version of his killer chili noodles and I carefully picked out the noodles, letting the crazy sauce drip off the chop sticks as much as possible.

As I went to bed that night, I realized that I had not thought of Tate all evening.

I was proud of myself. I was beginning to get a life outside of work, seeing new parts of the city and having fun.

This was what coming to the city was all about.

Even the crazy chili was a part of it.

Now I knew I didn't like it.

I couldn't wait to find out what else I didn't like.

Chapter 8

Tate

I had just gotten through a round of cardio when my phone rang.

I looked at the screen.

It was Star.

I groaned inwardly, grabbed a towel and wiped my face.

Just about the only thing we'd ever had in common was the fact that we both liked to get up early. The sun wasn't even up yet. But she'd have put on her make-up, straightened her hair and done her whole wardrobe. This was exercise according to Star, making sure none of her accessories clashed and that she had no lipstick on her teeth. Looking good was important to her professionally, she said no-one would hire a stylist who was either fat or too old or bad-looking. Of course, Star's definition of bad-looking was as big as the Grand Canyon. She could spend hours in front of the mirror, scrutinizing her skin, examining her pores or trying to get rid of new wrinkles she claimed had arrived overnight. She did hours of face yoga every day.

Face yoga! For goodness' sakes.

I answered the phone.

"Glad I caught you! I want to run something by you quickly," Star said in that breathless, girly way she had of talking. She'd always done it, but it seemed to have gotten worse since she moved to LA. The older she became, the younger she pretended to be.

"Go for it," I said, apprehension building. Summer had warned me after all.

"Trevor proposed and I said yes!!!" she suddenly cried over the phone.

"Congratulations," I said, because it was expected. "I hope you will be very happy."

"Thanks," she said, a little warmth in her voice.

"I want to invite you guys for a weekend here, you and Summer, to get to know Trevor and his son a little better."

"Have you met Summer?" I asked sarcastically, "She doesn't like anyone."

"I know," Star chuckled nervously. "That's why I want you guys to come out here. It's important that all of you get along. We'll be living together and if Summer comes to visit, she'll stay with us and I don't want things to be awkward."

"But you don't need me for that," I protested.

"But... I do," Star said, her voice wavering. I hated it when she did that.

"I'll never win over Summer on my own."

"You don't know that," I said. But I knew she was right.

"Summer hates me," Star said, her voice shaking. "I think she hates Trevor too."

Summer did hate Trevor, that much was true but I wasn't going to confirm it to Star. They had taken Summer to Disneyland one weekend in an effort to win her over and get her to warm to Trevor and his son, Adam. Summer had hated it, complaining non-stop about the heat and the people and the number of people coughing on her. She had come back telling me that she thought there was something seriously wrong with Trevor. "Like pathologically wrong, Dad. He's a psychopath!"

"He's a film executive, Summer," I said. "They're all like that. Ready to kill for the next big success."

"His studio makes terrible movies," she crinkled her face, like she smelled something rotten.

I almost felt sorry for the guy. Getting Summer to like you was an almost impossible task. The worst thing you could do was try too hard.

I thought of how easily Summer had taken to Evie and wondered again about that. I'd never seen her like anyone that fast.

"Can I bring someone?" I casually asked Star.

"Bring someone? What, like a girlfriend?" Star asked, totally surprised. I loved hearing that. She thought I was going to come all alone, watch her and Trevor hold hands, wave some shining rock in my face, flash their happiness and love in my face while I sat there, all alone and lonely.

"Yeah, you mind?" I was being all casual, enjoying winding her up.

"I didn't know you were seeing someone?" She sounded put-out, like I should have told her, boasting about it as she had done with me as soon as things got serious with Trevor.

"Actually, we're engaged," I said, surprising even myself.

"No! When did this happen?!"

Star sounded stunned.

"Summer didn't say!"

"Well, we've kept it quiet, you know."

Very quiet indeed, I thought, so quiet that nobody knew. Not even me, who was supposed be the one who was engaged. I didn't think it through, of course, I mean who would I bring? I would have to cancel right before the weekend, claiming a wax emergency or something. Women took those seriously.

"You must bring her!" Star sounded completely hyped up. So much warmth flooded her voice, it almost sounded real. "I just want you to be happy! And if you too have found love, well, that would just be the greatest!"

I rolled my eyes. "Uh-huh," I mumbled.

"Will you stay at our place in Malibu?" she enquired innocently.

"No, I think we'll find our own place," I said.

"Which weekend will suit you," she asked, rattling off dates and by the time I put down the phone, I had managed to book a weekend in LA for me, my daughter and my imaginary girlfriend, sorry, fiancée.

By the time Summer came down for breakfast, I was ready to tell her the news.

I waited for her to get something to eat and a glass of milk.

"I was talking to Star this morning," I started.

"And?" she put down her toast, staring at me. She knew what was coming.

"You were right," I said. "She's getting married to Trevor and she wants us to come out there and get to know him and his son."

"I know them already, thank you very much. Arseholes, both of them."

Case closed, according to Summer.

"Sweetheart, your mom is serious about this guy and she wants you to get along with him and the kid."

"The kid is, like, I don't know, creepy! I don't want anything to do with him!" Summer's voice was getting louder. I could see she was getting upset. To distract her and calm her down, I told her what I'd said about taking a fiancée along.

It worked.

"You did what?!" she cried out.

"Your mom was completely freaked out," I said.

"Of course she was! She thinks you're still totally in love with her!" she grinned.

As if I ever was. But that was a story for another time.

"What are you going to do?" Summer asked, giggling.

"Maybe I'll ask Evie to go along, pretend to be my fiancée for the weekend." Why not, I thought. A few days, what was the harm? She was my PA, her job was to assist me and this was how I needed assisting.

"Yes! Please do that, Dad, please!" I wasn't expecting Summer's response to be this strong. I had to laugh, "Okay, okay, I'll ask her."

"Evie's great," Summer said and went back to finishing her breakfast. I watched her, the anxiety of earlier had vanished. Summer seemed like a tough kid but it was all an act. She had been in therapy for years after the divorce and the therapist had said she needed stability and rules. That is why she'd come to live with me. When she was with Star, they were always moving around, going away on film sets whenever Star got a job doing make-up for a movie. It was only when she was with me that she seemed able to settle, sleep through the night and settle down. It didn't take much to convince Star to let Summer stay with me, it was clear to me that having to look after Summer was a bit of burden to her. She did love her, but she was so obsessed with getting her career on track after the divorce that everything came after that in her life, even her daughter. Even if I worked all day, at least at my house she had her own room, which always stayed the same. When we asked Summer, she'd said straight away she wanted to live with me.

I decided it would be better if I asked Evie in front of Summer, I had a feeling she would be able to help convince her. I was right.

"You want me to do what?" Evie had asked. I had just told her to move a few meetings and do some research on another project, then casually, I'd asked her if she'd go to LA with me and Summer for a weekend and pretend to be my fiancée.

"It's two days, three max," I said. "You'd really be helping us out."

"Yes, pleeeease," Summer chipped in, begging her too.

"Think about it!" I said, quickly leaving for a run before she could say no. I don't know what Summer said to her, but when I spoke to Evie later in the day, she told me in no uncertain terms that she was not happy about lying like this, but she would do it for Summer.

"We're not going to have sex or anything like that, right?" she asked.

Fortunately, we were on the phone, making this conversation a little easier.

"Not unless you want to?" I teased.

She ignored me, keeping her voice stern. "No kissing, no PDAs."

"But a little hand holding?" I was teasing her, of course.

"You wouldn't hold hands," she said quickly, almost too quickly.

She knew me so well, better than my ex-wife did, come to think of it.

"You'll come then?" I kept my voice light, to hide the excitement I was feeling.

"I guess so," she sighed.

I waited until the call was over before I let out a big whoop of celebration.

Chapter 9

E vie
"Wait!" I called after Tate, getting up from the kitchen counter where I was sitting and running after him.

"We need to talk about this!"

But he was already gone.

I walked back slowly to Summer, who was looking at me with a little smile.

"Come on," she said, making big puppy eyes at me. "Say you'll do it?"

I bit my lip. "I'm really uncomfortable with this Summer, can't you see?"

She looked down. "Why? It's just for two days?"

"Lying to your mom?"

"She lies all the time!" Summer cried out. "Like, you probably think she is a natural blonde! But her hair is really red, or a sort of orange color. She goes to this hairdresser every week and he nukes it into oblivion!"

"Well, that's not really lying," I said. "Everyone lies about stuff like that."

"You too?"

"Well..." I was wearing a push-up bra that made my breasts look a lot perkier and rounder than they actually were. I'd always been a bit embarrassed about their size and then I found a wonderful shop in the city that sold unbelievable underwear. It was hideously expensive but so worth it.

"So some lying is okay but other kind of lies aren't?" She asked me, lifting an eyebrow sarcastically.

Man, this girl was good.

"Yes," I said. "You will learn all about it when you grow up."

She closed her eyes.

"Don't you feel bad about lying to your mom, though?"

"You don't get it!" Summer yelled at me, flying into a sudden rage and running up to her room. I had to follow her even though I had never been upstairs before. Tate's house was a magnificent beachfront property built into a cliff and consisting of several levels. I didn't know how many there were, but I was guessing four or more. The first level was the kitchen and a kind of lounge area where I usually met him in the mornings to discuss the day. The next floor up was the bedrooms, I think. There was a gym below, and I was guessing a dining room and another more formal lounge too. Maybe a pool? But I'd never been beyond the kitchen area.

I went up after Summer and found myself on a huge floor with steps leading up to another level. I was guessing that the master bedroom would be on top. To be sure, I went up and entered a door from a narrow landing.

It took my breath away. It was a huge space, divided into a private lounge, a bathroom and the bedroom, with glass windows all around. There was a balcony too, facing the ocean and beachfront. The bed was huge but neatly made, there were no clothes lying around. It was the tidiest male bedroom I'd ever seen. I had a mental image of Tate walking across to take a shower in his bathroom, completely naked.

I quickly shut down that movie reel in my head.

I had to find Summer.

I went down a flight of stairs and went to one of the doors, but it was a guest bedroom. Not as big as the master suite, but still a generous space with quite a decent sea view. The other room was Summer's. I heard music come from behind the closed door.

"Summer? Can I come in?"

There was no answer. I knocked again and went in.

Summer was standing out on the balcony, the wind blowing her hair back. Her room was a mess, clothes strewn all over the floor, dirty dishes and towels, books and drawings scattered all over the place. I carefully picked my way through the chaos to join her outside.

"Summer?"

She didn't look at me and I went to stand next to her, looking out at the beach. There were people walking and a dog running and barking like crazy on the sand. We watched this happy scene for a while.

"I just... don't think it's right," I said.

"Why not, do you have a boyfriend?" Summer asked. "Do you think he'll be mad?"

"No," I said, "I don't have a boyfriend."

For a second, I thought of Xavier, who had kissed me a few nights ago after we'd gone out. It was a pleasant kiss but I hadn't felt much in the way of fireworks. He wanted to come inside and I said I had to get up early. He had been very downcast and Luisa teased me about him afterwards. I told her that I liked Xavier but only as a friend.

"Then date him as a friend," she had said with shrug. "Where's the harm in that?"

I pulled a face and she had looked at me closely.

"There is someone else, isn't there!"

"No," I had said, but too quickly.

She scrutinized my face, "Who is it? Is it that hunky boss of yours?"

I may have mentioned that he was good-looking in the beginning, after I had just started working there.

"He won't look at me twice," I countered.

"But you still like him?" she asked.

"Not like that," I said but she didn't believe me, I could tell.

Now Summer was looking at me too.

"If only me and Dad go, it will be three against two."

"What?"

"You know, her and Trevor and Adam against me and Dad. If you're there, it will be fair, we won't be outnumbered."

"You make it sound like a war!"

"It will be!" she swung to face me. "But not with bullets and guns, rather pina coladas and platters."

I frowned. "That doesn't sound too bad."

Summer smiled. "Then say you'll come with us."

Her sad little face and those big eyes looking at me, how could I say no?

"Okay," I said, rolling my eyes, and she threw her arms around me, giving me a big hug.

"Thank you! Thank you! Thank you!" she said, squeezing me tightly.

"It's just two days, right?" I laughed, wondering what I'd gotten myself into.

"Exactly! And you might enjoy it!"

"I've never been to LA," I said and I felt a spark of excitement then.

"Maybe you'll love it," Summer said.

"But you hate it?" I said.

She shrugged, "Not all of it, some parts are nice."

"Oh yeah, like which parts?"

I wanted to hear her say something nice about the city in which her mother lived. I wanted her to cheer up and think of positive things. And... I wanted to know if there was anything I could look forward to.

Summer thought for a bit.

"Venice beach is okay, I mean, I've gone roller skating there. And it's nice for ice cream."

"Oh, ice cream! You know I love ice cream!"

"I know!" Summer laughed. "And I like Malibu, it's okay, I guess."

I was beginning to look forward to this weekend.

Even though in the back of my mind, there was a little voice telling me not to be fooled by Summer's little face. This is a bad idea, the voice said. You're doing something you shouldn't be doing.

It wasn't just the lying. It was the pretending to be Tate's fiancée.

We would be close, spending a lot of time together, having to play the part of a romantic couple. It was dangerous, considering what had already happened between us and what I was trying very hard, not to have happen again.

So far, it was working. We were very professional and cordial to one another. Sometimes there would be a bit of a vibe and then we'd talk of something else, move away. He had not so much as accidentally touched me in weeks.

"Why me anyway?" I asked Summer. "Isn't your dad seeing Jacqueline? Why don't you guys take her along?"

Summer pulled a face. "I don't like her. She's stuck-up."

"Is she?" I pretended to be surprised but I was secretly pleased. Summer preferred me to the gorgeous Jacqueline.

"When she talks to me it's always in this weird voice, like she's talking to a four-year-old."

Summer put on a funny voice to imitate Jacqueline "Oh, look at the pretty drawing you made!"

She shook her head. "She'll do anything to get dad to like her. But he doesn't really."

I wanted to ask her more but I couldn't. I didn't want Summer to know that I had any interest in her father.

Because I didn't, not really.

I had to get rid of those feelings as soon as they cropped up, like weeds springing up where they were not supposed to be. I couldn't allow them to become bigger and stronger. Because then I would be unable to stop them from taking over. I didn't want that to happen. I didn't know if I'd be able to resist Tate if he tried to kiss me or touch me again. In fact, I knew I wouldn't. Going away for the weekend with him was probably an extremely stupid idea. But it was too late now. Summer was happy now, finally smiling again. I couldn't disappoint her by changing my mind. At least, that is what I told myself.

Chapter 10

Tate

I would have liked to take the Ferrari on the road to Los Angeles but we didn't have enough time for the road trip. It would have to wait for another time. Instead, we took a flight on the Thursday, taking a few days off work.

Evie was nervous, I could tell.

She'd had her hair done, plus some shopping with the help of my credit card, of course. I couldn't let her embarrass me in LA, she had to look the part of my fiancée after all. Summer and I dreamed up a career for Evie as a wealthy businesswoman. Evie didn't have much of a say in the matter, Summer and I worked everything out, making a game of it and enjoying ourselves quite a bit in the process.

At the airport, while we were waiting for our flight, with Summer listening to music on her headphones, I thanked Evie for doing this.

"I know you don't really want to."

She nodded. "Summer really wanted me to, I don't know why."

I checked to see that Summer was not listening to our conversation and dropped my voice even more. "You know what this is about?"

She shook her head.

"Summer is mad at her mom for doing the whole happy family thing now. She resents her for not wanting to be a family with us. She doesn't want to like Trevor and Adam because she feels it would be a betrayal of me."

Evie gave me a look. "I think you've watched too much Dr. Phil."

I had to laugh.

Evie said, "Maybe this Trevor really is a douchebag?"

"He is, actually," I had to admit. "But I do want Summer to be okay with him as her stepdad. If anything should happen to me, she'll have to live with them."

Evie nodded and I knew she got it.

She was looking very fetching with her new haircut and sexy sun dress. Summer and I had decided that she needed to be a bit more feminine in her outfits, and we forced Evie to buy a number of sun dresses that she said she felt very uncomfortable in. But she looked great, it took all my willpower not to grab her and kiss her.

But I knew I had to be careful with Evie this weekend. I didn't want to spook her. Even though I knew she was still attracted to me, she clearly had this idea in her head that it was not professional for us to fool around. I mean, who cares, I'm the boss and I make the rules, right?

But if she bolted now, the weekend was ruined and Summer would be disappointed.

I was sure, though, that somewhere on this weekend, I would find a moment to be alone with Evie and take up where we left off in the elevator lobby.

But I had not known what Star had up her sleeve.

The moment we landed in LA, we were taken on a whirlwind tour of the city. It was lunches in fancy restaurants, followed by dinner parties and clubbing on the first night. The second day, she came to pick up Summer and Evie from the hotel for a day of shopping while I tried to get some work done. I barely had a moment to myself with Evie. I could see Star was determined to make my supposed fiancée love her and Evie was going along with it. On Friday night, there was a party at some film studio executive's house in the Hills and Summer stayed with a babysitter while Evie and I went out. Evie looked fantastic in a dress that hugged every curve. She complained about how she could barely move in it and when I told her it was worth it, she held up a warning finger, "Stop it! None of that."

I had to hold my horses.

At the house, I plied her with one drink after another, hoping she would loosen up but instead, she got drunk and fell asleep in the car on the way back. I was beginning to think our moment would never come.

But then, a stroke of luck.

Star was called out to an emergency. A celebrity with a style crisis. It happened on the Saturday when we were supposed to go for brunch. Star came by to the hotel to apologize in person.

"I am so sorry," she said. "I just can't say no. I mean Julia is such a big star, you know, right?"

I didn't, of course, I didn't know half of these so-called celebrities, but Evie immediately said, "Of course! She is huge! And she's got that new movie coming out, right?"

"Right!" Star was relieved to see Evie got it. "She's got this lunch to go to and she has to look hot, but apparently her skin is all blotchy..." Star looked around to check no-one was listening, then she dropped her voice like she was a CIA agent or something and muttered, "From a procedure, you know, bad reaction..." she lifted her eyebrows and stared pointedly, to get the point across.

"Anyway, I said I'd do something with her hair, you know, try and cover it."

"Of course!" Evie was nodding enthusiastically when Star suddenly said, "Why don't you come along? You can help me, be my assistant!"

I interjected, "Star, please, you can't expect that of Evie, she's a professional businesswoman, not some make-up artist!"

But Evie surprised me, saying, "No, I'd love that, truly!"

I was going to take Summer to see Adam and Trevor at the house and in the evening, we would pick up Star and Evie from Julia's place in Bel-Air.

That had been the plan, at least.

I spent a day of excruciating boredom at Trevor's house, listening to him drone on about movies and Superhero franchises and how demanding his job was. Summer and Adam seemed to get on just fine over the PlayStation and I excused myself to make a few phone calls, leaving them for a few hours to get away for a bit.

Late in the afternoon, I got a strange call from Evie.

"Oh, my God!" she was gushing, "You should see this place. And Julia is so lovely! Her face is not that bad at all!"

"Are you okay?" I asked. Evie sounded a bit spacey.

"I'm a-ok!" she sang.

"Did you take something?" I asked.

"Just champagne," she started saying, then laughingly added, "A glass or three or maybe four! I've been swimming in the pool while Star is in there with Julia." Her voice dropped. "There are all these people here, actors and models, just... hanging out, I guess."

I was getting a bit worried.

"Listen, I'll come get you, okay? Have you eaten?" I had a feeling Evie was a bit out of her depth there, surrounded by the glitz of Hollywood. I knew Star took all kinds of upper and downers and inbetweeners, and mixing that with alcohol was not a good idea. Evie told me she was fine and in the afternoon, when the client went out to her lunch, I stopped by to pick up Star and Evie.

I pressed the buzzer to the house and the door opened. I could hear laughter coming from the pool area and made my way through a hacienda-type house to an outdoor pool where people were swimming and drinking and clearly having a party. I looked for Evie and finally found her in the pool, stark naked.

"Evie?"

"Hey there, lover!" she called out to me, sounding very cheery. "Come over here!" she was trying to pull me into the swimming pool but I evaded her. "Where is Star?"

"She went home."

"Without you?" I found that hard to believe.

"I told her I wanted to stay, said you'd come pick me up," she batted her eyelids coquettishly at me.

"Hey man, leave her. She's having fun," some young guy said to me. He looked about sixteen years old, but underneath the eye tuck and a bit of lifting of the cheekbones, he was probably closer to forty.

"That is my fiancée you're talking about," I said sternly to him. "Back the fuck off!"

Evie got out of the pool and came towards me, dripping wet and giggling. Water running off her luscious body, her hair wet against her skin. It was an enchanting sight. I'd not had a chance to look at her properly that night in the office and here she was, running naked towards me. I opened my arms and she walked into them.

"I'm having the best time," she whispered into my shirt.

"Are you really?" I asked her. "I have a feeling you might feel differently about this in the morning?"

"Who cares about tomorrow, right?" She stole a look at me between wet lashes, pressing her wet body against me, sending me a very clear message of her intentions. I wasn't going to let this opportunity pass me by. I quickly got her dressed and drove us back to our hotel room, calling Trevor and arranging that Summer spend the night at their place. I couldn't wait to get Evie alone at the hotel room and the door had barely closed behind us when we were kissing and grabbing at each other's clothes, trying to get into bed as quickly as possible.

"This is probably not a good idea," Evie giggled as she took off my shirt.

"This is a wonderful idea," I said as ripped her t-shirt off and kissed her, tasting the unbelievable sweet Evie again.

"I promised myself I wasn't going to do this," Evie said a little later, kissing my chest and licking my skin, smiling naughtily at me.

"I'm delighted you decided to break that promise," I whispered to her as I opened her legs and entered her, feeling the most exquisite pleasure at the wonderful wetness between her thighs.

Chapter 11

E vie
       I wake up with the hangover from hell.

It is the worst hangover I've ever had.

There have been a few of those, I'm not proud to say. When I was a kid, I once got drunk with my brothers. They weren't paying attention and I was drinking beers on the sly, trying to keep up with them. I ended up puking my guts out in the garden and they got an earful from my mother and I didn't go to school the next day, too sick to move. Once, in college, I had underestimated the power in a punch bowl at a friend's housewarming party and had passed out on their porch, waking up half-frozen in the middle of the night, spending a few confusing moments trying to figure out where the hell I was.

But this was worse.

Much, much worse.

There was the headache and the nausea, as well as a body ache that made it almost impossible to get up and walk to the bathroom. Then, added to that, was the shame of what had happened the night before. Because, the moment I got out of bed and saw that I was naked, it all came flooding back.

Me at Julia-what's-her-name's house, taking pills and drinking while Star worked and then, for some unfathomable reason, taking off my clothes and swimming naked with a bunch of people who kept smiling at me and telling me they loved me and how beautiful I was. Then Tate came and I think I told him he was beautiful and I loved him. Or I wanted to make love to him. I had the sinking feeling that is what I said to him and then not long after that, we did that. A few times, as I recall.

There was a note next to the bed saying he had gone to fetch Summer and that I should take some aspirin. He'd left out two tablets, which I gratefully drank with water. Then I got back into bed and groaned a bit, it made me feel better.

How could I have been so stupid?

Why had I gone with Star, why did I take drugs and drink champagne in the middle of the day? I guess part of it was being blinded by going to a film star's house and hanging out there like it was normal. And I'd never taken any kind of drug before and I wanted to try it, to see what it was like to be one of those gorgeous people who smiled at everyone and looked lovely and were so awesome to have around, like stunning house plants or charming pets.

But that wasn't me.

I felt terrible.

I fell asleep and woke up a little while later, to the sound of someone knocking on the door.

"Evie? It's Star."

I went to open the door.

Tate's ex-wife handed me a big shaker and told me to drink it.

"Don't look at it," she warned me. "Don't smell it either! Just pinch your nose like this," she showed me. "And drink it."

I was too weak to argue. I drank it while Star told me that Tate had decided to go golfing with Trevor. Summer and Adam were having a rematch of some game they'd been playing.

"At least they're getting along," she said, rolling her eyes as if exasperated, but I knew she was pleased they were getting on.

"I felt bad when I heard how you were feeling," she said, making big eyes. "I thought you were all right yesterday?"

"It's all an act," I said, wondering if she knew how much of it was true. "I don't have a clue what I'm doing half the time."

Her eyes narrowed. "But Tate said you were such a smart businesswoman! He was, like, totally in awe of how you apparently won over your board to go global with your business."

Typical Tate, I thought. Overdoing the praise.

"Yeah, well. He's pussy whipped I guess."

That prompted a laugh from Star. She looked at me differently all of a sudden. Until then, I'd had an uncomfortable feeling from her, like she was always trying to size me up, or figure me out. Even when we were out on the job at Julia's house, she wasn't completely relaxed around me.

"I've been withholding sex," I said, making it up as I went along. "I guess it's working."

"Why?" she asked, leaning forward.

"It's a bit awkward," I said. "We've been arguing about things and I guess, I'm punishing him."

"I get it," she said, nodding her head energetically. "Keep him keen. It's the same with me and Trevor. Although he can be a little too keen, if you know what I mean," she gave a high-pitched laugh that sent shockwaves of pain through my head. She tossed her hair back and winked at me.

The thought of Trevor being enthusiastic in bed was not appealing. It made me want to throw up. His bald head, the huge belly, the fleshy nose on that guy. The thought of him naked made me rush to the bathroom.

"You okay?" Star stood in the doorway, her voice full of fake concern. I had puked out all of her miracle shake.

"I'm sorry I'm being such a bore," I croaked but she smiled at me and I could see she was loving this. Seeing me reduced to this miserable state. It made me feel a bit sad for her, that this would make her feel better. She had to feel awful about herself to need to see me humbled like this. But oddly enough, I didn't mind. "I'm glad Summer is having a good time, she was anxious about this weekend."

A calculating look passed over Star's face and I thought for a moment I had overplayed my hand.

"So, when is the wedding?" she asked sweetly.

"I don't know if there will be a wedding now," I said weakly. "Tate was really mad at me for getting so wasted. He stormed out of here this morning in such a state."

Star came closer. "He can be controlling, you have to watch out."

I nodded. "I know, I know." I wanted to win Star over but even more than that, I wanted to sleep. "You've been really wonderful Star, but I think I'm going to lie down now," I said, stumbling to bed.

"Get better soon, hon," she smiled at me with perfect teeth and plump pink lips. When I woke up again, it was evening but Tate was still not back.

At least, I felt better.

I got dressed and went down for something to eat. I carefully walked to the elevator, feeling soreness in my thighs. I had a memory of slinging them over Tate's shoulder at one point in the evening, why was I even attempting a position like that? I must have been out of my mind.

But at the same time, I couldn't help wondering at how natural it had felt between us, how easy it was. When he'd arrived at the party and I had come on to him, he had responded with such enthusiasm, like he had been waiting for me to show him a sign that I wanted him, that I wanted to sleep with him again. He had ripped off my clothes with such impatience in the hotel room, and he'd initiated sex again and again after that. Not that I minded, I mean, Tate was attractive and attentive and he was as focused on giving me pleasure as getting off himself. And I'd been trying to push away the thoughts of him for so long that it was wonderful just giving in and letting us enjoy each other's bodies.

And we did, oh boy, did we ever.

I had had sex before, but not like this.

What I had done before amounted to fumbling in the dark, boys not really knowing what they were doing. But Tate knew what he was doing. How to touch me, tease me, make me want more.

Nobody had ever looked at my body like he did, caressing it like it was a thing of beauty, licking and kissing me all over. Nibbling on my ear, licking me between my legs, just the thought of it sent shivers down my spine.

I thought of the sex I'd had with my ex-boyfriend, Colin. He was a friend of my brother's and we went out for a few years, my last year of school and in college. We would see each other over weekends, making out in his car, or at his parents' house, having to be as quiet as possible so they didn't hear anything. The whole experience took about two minutes and we often had to stop in the middle, freezing, listening for a creak on the stairs that would signify his mom coming up to check on us. It was hardly a romantic setting.

After college, after Colin and I broke up, I saw another guy at the lake for a few weeks. Sex with him was strange. He had issues about his dick begin too small and wouldn't let me look at it or touch it. He'd try and enter me and come as quickly as he could. As far as I could tell, he was pretty normal looking in that department but he would never believe me and I think that was one of the big reasons why he stopped calling me. Not that I minded. It was bad enough that he had hang ups about his dick, I didn't want to start having hang ups about it.

But with Tate, everything happened the way it should. There were no problems, there was no weirdness. There was this insane energy between us and I was convinced he felt it like I did, it connected us and we were on the same wave length.

It was great but also confusing, because what did that mean?

I was still his PA and he was still my boss. We couldn't be together in any way, that wouldn't work at all.

Chapter 12

Tate

The drive to Malibu is a weird one.

I've driven the road many times before, but this time it's like a surrealistic movie or one of those indie films people rave about that is a nightmare to sit through. When I leave the hotel, I feel good, euphoric even, after the night with Evie. It was everything I'd wanted it to be, all I'd been fantasizing about for weeks. She was so ready for me, wanting it every bit as much as I had. It was just like I'd thought, she was more than willing and had tried to stop it from happening because she thought it wasn't right.

The sex was incredible. She was so beautiful, her body was soft like ripe fruit and I wanted to devour every inch of it. I had spent hours exploring her body and what joy to find out her erogenous zones, the moans of desire that a nibble on her ear or the stroking of her belly button could elicit.

But then, a few miles down the road, I started thinking about the future. What would happen now? Was she going to become one of those women who wanted to date, go out for romantic evenings? Was I in for long discussions of feelings and futures and expectations? Evie was young, after all, quite possibly she wanted marriage and children and the happy ever after. I wasn't ready for that. Or rather, I was over that. I'd had that with Star and it had imploded rather dramatically.

By the time I reached Trevor's house, I was in a foul mood.

What if I had opened a Pandora's box of terrible things? Had I ruined a wonderful PA with one, maybe two nights, of mind-blowing sex? Was it worth it? How could it be?

"Hey dad," Summer said casually when she saw me.

I couldn't believe how laid-back she was being.

Did it really only take a few hours of GTA with her potential stepbrother to bring her round to her mother's way of thinking? Of course, when I quizzed her later in the car, the real story came out. They'd made a bet, the winner of the game would be able to call the shots in their relationship and of course, Star had won. This meant that if they ever moved, she would get to choose the best bedroom and could always sit in front in the car, riding shot gun. She was in fine spirits.

"What about your mom?" I asked.

"She's been more into Evie than me," Summer said with a big grin. "Every time we've been together she's been all, who's this Evie, how long has your dad been seeing her, etc., etc."

She added, "She's so jealous, dad, it's incredible!"

"Huh," was all I could say.

"Even Trevor noticed," Summer said. "He asked me if I thought it was serious between the two of you."

"What did you say?"

"I said I didn't know," she giggled. Then she became serious.

"But... Dad?"

"Yeah?"

"You do kinda like her, right?"

I blinked. "What do you mean?"

"Like, I get the feeling you do like her?"

Jesus, this girl, she was too smart for her own good, I thought.

"She's my PA, Summer," I said instead.

"But I wouldn't mind, you know," she said. "If you wanted to, you know, date her."

"Date her?" Here we go again, I thought.

"She's better than those other women, like Jacqueline or whatever."

I thought about Jacqueline and all the messages she'd left on my mobile. How I was, when we'd go out again, what I was up to. It drove me insane. I had responded to none of them. Would Evie end up just like that, I wondered. I had a feeling she might.

"Look, I'm not sure all that relationship stuff is for me," I started.

"It's okay, dad," Evie interrupted. "I'm just saying, I like Evie. A lot. She's cool."

We drove back to the hotel and Summer said she wanted to go to a shop she'd heard about first. I didn't mind a little diversion before we got back to the hotel. I had a feeling Evie would be feeling very hungover and possibly emotional after our night together.

I didn't feel too great about it myself, come to think of it.

We had one more day of LA left to go and yet I was ready to go home. The City of Angels always had this effect on me, making me wish I'd never come here.

"So, what do you think of Star and Trevor?"

Summer shrugged. "They're okay. They tried hard to make things nice for me."

I thought about how Star had made me coffee when I came to fetch Summer. She was dressed in tiny shorts with a tank top, the way she'd dressed when I met her as a young woman. It made me think of the Star I used to know, the way things had been between us when it was still good, before a baby and the shock of adulthood slammed into our faces.

I knew I was hard on Star, the way I was hard on most people, even myself.

"I like Evie," Star had said, as I was sipping my coffee.

"Good," I said.

"She's young," she said carefully. "But not too young," she'd added.

"Trevor is a bit old," I'd said. "But probably not too old."

Star laughed. "You always were a bit of an arsehole."

I laughed too. "Not just a bit. A lot, I hope."

She shook her head. "You're the only guy I know who would want to be called an arsehole!"

"It's because it's honest. I don't care about pleasing people, I do what I want and like it or not, that is who I am."

She nodded, poured herself some water from a special urn with leaves and seeds floating around in it.

"Trevor and I have been going to this couples therapist ahead of the wedding? He is an Eastern philosophy guru, very much into healing the inner child to become a fulfilled adult."

I thought of my inner child and what it wanted.

I didn't think giving ten-year-old me any airtime would be good for my adult self. I remember myself being quite a little shit at that age, going around pranking my brother, trying to scare my mother and giving her and my father much to think about. I was constantly in trouble, trying to break the rules, push boundaries. For my father, the lawyer, and my mother, a homemaker, I was a bit of a mystery. Why couldn't I be a good boy like my brother? Just do what was expected of me? At some point, I thought it was expected of me to be the bad boy. Of course, then I got suspended from school and had to finish high school at a notorious city public school where I got to deal with different kinds of problems.

Star was oblivious to what was going on in my head.

"The therapist said we needed to love ourselves, to give ourselves the attention our parents never gave us."

Such crap. I knew Star's parents, they were lovely people. Ordinary, decent, it wasn't their fault that Star, much like me, had wanted more out of life than they could give her. She, just like me, had rebelled against the order of her universe. It had gotten her into more trouble than she should have been. But Star was pretty and skinny, with an attractive pout that caught the boys' attention early on. She knew how to use it too, partnering it with a sidelong glance from heavily-mascaraed eyes. Worked like a charm.

"Do you love Trevor?"

"Love is a very Western concept and it has come to mean so many different things," she said, all serious, and I had to stop myself from laughing out loud. "We are thinking more of ourselves as two separate parts coming together," she said in a sing-song voice.

"Like slices of bread in a sandwich?" I asked innocently.

A pained look came over her face. "That's typical of you Tate, trying to break down what you don't understand."

But I didn't want to fight with her.

"I'm glad you and Trevor are happy," I said.

By the time I'd left with Summer, my mood had changed again. I wasn't sure what I was feeling now, but I didn't like it.

I was walking around the shops, waiting for Summer, when Evie called me.

"Where are you guys?" Evie asked.

"Summer is looking for some shop she heard about from Adam," I said.

There was a moment of silence when neither of us spoke. The silence felt heavy, expectant. Like we were waiting to hear something. At the same time we started talking,

"So,..." I said when she said,

"I was think..."

Then I said, "How're you feeling?"

"Shitty," she said.

Conversation didn't flow, we struggled to find the words to talk to each other.

"Maybe I should give you some space to feel better?" I suggested.

I had no idea what I meant exactly, or maybe I did.

She was quiet for a bit and then she said, "Maybe that's a good idea."

I put down the phone with a strangely flat feeling in my stomach.

When Summer and I got back to the hotel room, there was a note from Evie saying there was a crisis back at the office and that she'd left to go fix it. She'd see me back in San Francisco.

"She just left?" Summer said, staring at me.

"I know this client, they can be very difficult," I said in Evie's defense. I was relieved, I couldn't deny it. She had given both of us a way out of a tricky situation. We could have a bit of a think about how to handle this. At least, that was what I thought.

Chapter 13

E vie
Is it a break up if you were never together?

This is the question that bothers me over the next few days. Ever since that phone call and the flight back to San Francisco, I am plagued by thoughts of it being all over between us. There can be no denying the awkwardness of that phone conversation we'd had on the last day. He did not want to be talking to me, I could hear it. He was freaked out by what had happened, no other way of putting it.

I couldn't call him out on it as he was my boss. I had nothing to gain from challenging him or upsetting him. I wanted to keep my job but it was increasingly looking like that was not going to happen. I had feelings for Tate Sagarro, I might as well admit it. Even if I was going to hide it.

Fortunately, he had a conference in Reno the rest of the week and we could avoid each other, communicating via text messages. I did go to Summer's swim meet as I'd promised her the week before. Just because things between her father and I were weird did not mean that I had to push her away.

"You came!" She threw her arms around me and hugged me tightly. "You were amazing!"

I told the nanny to take the night off, that I would give Summer her dinner and spend the night.

"Are you sure?" The nanny was an au pair from Sweden who'd been travelling around the US until she ran out of money. She had a tempestuous relationship with the drummer of a moderately successful band and they were always breaking up and getting back together.

Whenever I wanted to feel good about my being single, I asked her about her relationship with Tank, as the boyfriend was called.

"They're playing at Los Lamas tonight," Annika said. "I'd love to see them."

"It's fine, really." It was too, I liked spending time with Summer. We would watch Real Housewives, eat junk food and I'd spend the night in the guest room. As I put her to bed that night, making sure she brushed her teeth the full two minutes, she asked me suddenly, "Did you and Dad have a fight?"

"Why do you ask?"

"You haven't been around all week and when I asked him about it, Dad was all weird about it."

"Like how?" I wanted to hear what she'd say.

"I don't know, like, weird," she shrugged.

"I guess we did, yeah," I said. It was a kind of fight. The kind where nobody yelled or used bad language, but it was still bad between you.

"I bet it's all his fault," Summer said. "You're just too nice."

I smiled at her. "Sometimes it's nobody's fault. Stuff just happens."

She made a sad face. "As long as you'll still be my friend."

"Always," I said, giving her a hug.

But it didn't feel right being in Tate's house. After Summer went to bed, I wandered around looking at photographs of him and Star when they were younger. I snooped through his drawers, looking at bills. In his study, I checked some of his notebooks, looked at drawings he made of who-knew-what. There was so much of the man that was a mystery to me, I had no idea what he was thinking about most of the time. I wandered downstairs into the gym, looked at all the equipment and got tired just looking at the weights.

Finally, I went into his bedroom, touched his perfectly ironed shirts, the rows of sneakers. I checked his night table and found books about adventurers, explorers as well as drawings that Summer had made when she was younger. The fact that he had kept them said a lot. I couldn't bear being in his bedroom anymore. He was everywhere here, his smell and his presence surrounded me.

I quickly went downstairs and found some wine and opened my phone, scrolling around mindlessly until I was tired enough to go to sleep.

I decided to go home for the weekend.

It was my dad's birthday and my brother Andrew was coming down from DC to spend the weekend with our folks. I hadn't seen my eldest brother for quite a long time and I didn't want to miss out on a big family get together. I rented a car and drove to the cabin on Friday night, arriving as my father and my brothers were building a fire for the barbeque. Andrew was ten years older than me, when my parents moved to Lake Tahoe, he was seventeen years old and about to finish high school. He'd stayed in the city while Steve and I had moved out to the lake with my parents. We didn't see each other often, usually at Christmas and Thanksgiving. He'd gone to college in the capitol and worked as a lawyer for a big NGO advocating against gender violence. My parents were very proud of him.

"Little sis!" he called out as soon as he saw me walking up from the car.

He scooped me up in his arms for a warm hug. We stood around the fire in the backyard, drinking beer, listening to Steve telling us stories about the antics the tourists got up to on the boat, laughing even if the stories weren't that funny. I helped my mom in the kitchen and she touched my cheek.

"I'm so glad you came, I didn't know if you could get away," she said. "It feels great to have everyone together for a change."

And it was good to be around my family, where I didn't have to think about what I should say, or how I should act.

"So, what's it like working for Tate Sagarro?" Andrew asked me. "I mean, he's famous, right? One of those Silicon Valley nutters."

Everyone was looking at me, for once, interested in my opinion.

"It's actually pretty great," I admitted. "I thought he was batshit crazy in the beginning." Everyone laughed. "I still think he's crazy, but I'm beginning to see how his mind works. How he has to shut himself away to see the solutions he has to visualize."

They were watching me. "I mean people see the wacky side of him, the guy who tries to break speed records and they think he's chasing something he'll never find. And maybe he is, but he's always pushing boundaries, trying to find new ways of doing things."

"I have that app of his on my phone," Andrew said, talking about one of HumanIty's biggest sellers. "It has made my life so much easier."

"I hope this guy doesn't let you near his car," Steve said and everyone laughed again. Steve had taught me to drive and I had driven my dad's truck into the side wall a few times while learning how to park.

"I actually drove his Porsche to the dealer when he sold it," I said, very matter-of-fact.

"Bullshit!"

Steve wouldn't believe me, until I told him about the tiny space in the car.

"The Ferrari is much bigger," I said and Andrew's mouth literally hung open.

For the first time, I wasn't just their annoying little sister, but someone they wanted to listen to, whose stories they found fascinating. It was cool.

The next morning, I woke up early and joined my mom in the kitchen for an early coffee. The boys had already left for a fishing trip with my dad.

"I'm glad we have some girl time," my mom said, squeezing my hand.

"How is it really going at the new job?"

My mom's caring, kind words were enough to bring down the wall I had built around myself. I had no defenses against that.

"I love it," I said simply.

"And LA? What was that like? We've hardly spoke about that since you've come back?"

"What can I say, it was drugs, sex and rock 'n roll!"

"Really?!" My mother was suitably scandalized and couldn't wait to hear all the details.

"And what about a man? Is there someone?"

I was dying to talk about Tate and decided to tell her an edited version.

"Actually..."

My mother started clapping her hands in excitement. "I knew it! I knew it! This calls for cappuccinos!!!"

My mom's idea of a cappuccino came in a sachet and cost a dollar at the local store. It was hardly the work of art I had gotten used to at the office, produced by a machine the size of a small car. But my mother's cappuccinos tasted of home and acceptance and the kind of warmth that came with fitting in and being loved no matter what you did. That made it the best coffee in the world. I told her that there was a senior guy at the office that I had become friendly with, and had kissed one night. It was a very PG, scaled-down version of what had actually happened.

"Is he married?" she asked.

"No!" I was surprised that she'd even ask that.

"A lot older?"

"Yeah, a bit," I admitted

"Enjoy it while you can, but don't let it become too serious," she advised. "Before you know it, you'll be picking up his stinky underwear from your bathroom floor while he is playing videogames all night with his buddies." She was basically describing my brother Steve.

I pulled a face and she laughed.

But I would've loved to pick up Tate's jocks from my bathroom floor.

I couldn't tell her that though.

Because then it would be obvious that I'd fallen for him. Maybe just a small, tiny bit. Nobody needed to know.

But I knew, of course.

Chapter 14

Tate

I spend a week schmoozing with investors, talking tech at the convention, going out at night and partying with whoever invites me for drinks. I spend time at roulette tables, with strippers pushing their titties in my face and talk to big men with loud voices about money they don't have that they pretend they want to give to me. I give them the attention they want, spend time with people I would normally not even look at twice, all because I don't want to think about Evie.

But I can't have her in my head, filling the precious space with thoughts of her sweet face and juicy thighs. I had let it go to too far, had compromised myself with her. I thought it was just sex but the chemistry between us was powerful and the connection was too strong. She'd slipped past my internal firewall and was wreaking havoc with my code.

She'd hacked my emotions.

And there was only one way of dealing with a hacker. You had to shut them down. Find the weak chink in the armor, the code that gives it all away.

When I got back from Reno, I was exhausted. I thought I might sleep for two full days. Then I heard that she'd been here, with Summer, while I was away. Suddenly I saw her everywhere, I imagined her in my bed, sleeping alone and it drove me wild with desire. I pictured her naked of course, my satin sheets pulled over her perfect breasts.

"Where was Annika?" I asked Summer.

"With the band, of course," she rolled her eyes.

I made a mental note to fire her. She should have known better than to abandon my daughter.

"Don't fight with her too!" Summer warned me.

"What do you mean?"

"You and Evie, she said you'd had a fight."

"She said that?" That was an interesting take on our situation, I thought.

"Anyone could see something was going on, ever since LA," Summer said, knowingly. "Trevor said he thought she wanted to get married and you wouldn't, something like that." Summer laughed thinking about it, the whole weekend of Evie pretending she was my fiancée. Doing a brilliant job of it too, I had to say. The weekend was a success, mostly because of her. She'd taken the focus from everyone around her, making it easier for us to get on with the business of getting to know each other better.

"So what did you fight about?" Summer asked.

I had to tell her something, but nothing jumped to mind.

"Oh, you know, something silly."

"Did she forget to give you an important message?" Summer said.

"It was a very important message!" I blurted out, thinking this was as good an excuse as any.

"I lost a big potential client because she wanted to leave early and forgot to tell me about calling back this person!" I thought a bit. "And when I confronted her, she said she was sorry but that it wasn't such a big deal, which showed me how seriously she took her job and me as her boss!"

Summer was thoughtful. "That wasn't right."

"Exactly." I was glad to be vindicated.

"But... you said Evie is good at her job?"

"She is, she is," I said. "It was a silly fight. We'll make up again," I reassured her, but I didn't know if that was true. I'd already told Jill I wanted to start looking for another PA. I'd have to wait a while as I was going on a trip to the UK and wanted Evie to manage things while I was away, there was no time to train up a new PA. But I knew we couldn't work together anymore. I would have to face her sooner or later, tell her something. I wasn't looking forward to that.

My trip to London was important, I was looking at a collaboration with a big software development agency there and I needed to be sharp for the pitch. I couldn't afford to screw this up. The trip was in two weeks' time.

Then, out of the blue, I got a mail from my old college buddy, Felix Baumgarten.

He was from Germany and had spent a term at my college on an exchange program. We had clicked instantly. Even though he could hardly speak English and had an annoying way of always doing his work and trying to please the professors, we'd gotten along like a house on fire. After he went back to Germany to work for Google in Berlin, we'd stayed in touch.

He told me he was coming to California for work and he wanted to know if we could meet up. The last time I'd seen him, was in Italy a few years ago, when he'd invited me for a week on a yacht, cruising around the Mediterranean. By then, he'd left Google and was working for a major telecoms outfit, heading up the European division.

I told him I'd love to see him and I'd organize some snowboarding for us. The weather was turning, we were properly into Fall. Felix had grown up in the mountains, skiing and snowboarding were like running and walking to him.

I told Evie to go to the airport to pick Felix up and bring him home, give him the keys to one of the cars and tell him to make himself at home.

Felix was like a brother to me, I told her.

This was not entirely true, because I had a brother that I never saw and wasn't close to. My real brother, Brett, wasn't even that far away, only over in Napa Valley where he and his wife grew grapes and had three little boys who looked exactly like their father.

No, Felix and I were properly close.

I was looking forward to seeing him.

I sent Evie the details of the flight and when it was landing, telling her to take the Ferrari to pick him up.

That was the last time I thought about it.

I spent the afternoon in a board meeting, trying to convince the board to give me the money I needed to expand our marketing and increase our budget for experimentation. It was like getting blood out of a stone, but by the end of the meeting, I had gotten them to agree to a basic monetary commitment.

I drove home, looking forward to seeing Felix and spending time with him.

But when I got home, I immediately saw that I had other problems.

Felix and Evie were sitting on the coach, laughing and chatting much too intimately for my liking. It hadn't even occurred to me that this might be a problem. Of course, Felix was attractive. A tall Nordic God, with a big smile and a very cultivated and well-mannered personality.

When they noticed my arrival, both of them jumped up, looking very guilty.

"Tate! My man! How are you?" Felix came up to me, stretching out his hand to shake mine, but then pulling me into a hug. "It's been too long! But thank you for sending the Excellent Evie to come pick me up."

"Yeah, thanks Evie," I said without looking directly at her.

"No problem, I'll be off then," Evie said, grabbing her handbag and practically running for the door.

"Enjoy the catching up."

"You're not staying for dinner?" Felix said, visibly disappointed.

"I can't, so sorry," she said with an apologetic smile. "I am sure I will see you again soon."

"I hope so!" Felix said.

I waited for Evie to go before telling Felix about the gourmet meal the executive chef had planned for us for the evening.

"Sounds fantastic," Felix beamed at me.

I poured us some whiskey and he told me about work, about how stressed he was these days, his dreams of crashing and falling, of dying a million different ways, each and every night.

"But tell me," he said, suddenly leaning in.

"Your personal assistant, Evie?"

"Yeah? What about her?"

"Would you mind if I made a move on her?"

"A move?" I pretended not to know what he was talking about.

"She is gorgeous! I'd love to take her out."

Felix was in town for a few nights and I'd told him that I would not be able to entertain him every night. Seemed like he was very capable of making his own entertainment arrangements.

"I think she has a boyfriend," I said vaguely.

"But you don't have a problem with it?" He asked again, pressing the point.

Maybe he had a feeling something was going on, or it was the way Evie had stiffened when she'd seen me, clamming up and wanting to run out of there as fast as she could. A blind person could have seen there was something going on between me and her.

"Of course not," I said. "If you want to go for it, go for it!" I grinned at him, to show that I was really fine with it.

But inside, I was seething. Who did he think he was, thinking of putting his moves on her?

Evie was mine.

If I couldn't play with her, nobody could.

Chapter 15

E vie
    I'm in the middle of another odd job for Tate.

He's asked me to check out a female developer that Jill wants to hire. He got a weird vibe from her during the interview though. Seriously, he called it "a weird vibe". But she is highly qualified, has a good professional background and superb references. But the "weird vibe" bothers him. He wants me to check her out, see what my impressions about her are.

"Do you want to know if I get a 'weird vibe' off her?" I ask him, barely changing my tone of voice.

But he hears the sarcasm, and ignores it.

"Yes, precisely."

We've been having calls in the morning now, he calls me when he drives to work or goes off surfing. I go to work earlier, to ensure I'm at the computer when he rings. We're not talking face to face at the moment, and we haven't since LA. I have a feeling he's going to fire me. I've been looking at jobs online, playing around with the wording on my CV but secretly hoping that this job does work out after all.

I mean, in how many jobs are you asked to spend hours online trying to build a psychological profile of someone? Also, I know Tate likes oddballs, the weirdos and the nerds who got teased at school because they understood quantum physics but couldn't figure out basic cafeteria social rules. But he didn't want the kind of weird that would go psychopathic if they weren't picked for a project, people so isolated and lonely, they'd become fixated with someone at work. It was not an easy project.

This girl, Corinne Lassiter, was not easy to figure out. I'd watched the interview, which had been recorded and I knew what Tate meant. She was distant, a bit cool almost to the point of being rude. Stand offish. She didn't come across as desperate for the job, but there were small tells in her face, little tics that gave me the idea she really wanted the job but was hiding it well.

But I wasn't sure. I was trying to learn more about her from her social media posts but she hardly posted anything. She commented on other people's posts though and this was all I had to go on for now. I noticed someone coming into the office and looked up. It was Felix, tall and blonde, grinning at me.

"Hey, is Tate here?"

I looked at the time. "He's still in a meeting with some dev guys, did you guys have a date?" I didn't recall seeing it on his diary and he hadn't said anything to me.

"No, my meeting finished earlier and I thought we could go for lunch?"

"Oh, he doesn't eat lunch."

Felix looked at me with a frown. "We had a huge meal last night?"

I nodded. "He broke his fast last night, but today it's back on. Then he has one meal a day. Today was breakfast."

Felix shook his head. "What, two seeds and a spoon of oats?"

I laughed. "And two eggs!"

"Why?"

"He says it clears his mind, keeps him focused."

Felix shook his head, "Sounds like starvation to me!" I agreed with him but I didn't want to say it out loud. The mere thought of going without food for something like twenty hours was enough to make me faint with hunger.

"You don't do fasting?" I asked him.

"I love food too much," he said, patting his very flat and probably toned tummy. Then he said, "Then how about we go for lunch?"

I couldn't see why not.

"What do you feel like?" I asked him.

He shrugged. "Somewhere close, somewhere nice."

I grabbed my bag and we headed out.

I liked being with Felix, he was easy-going and very laid-back. I couldn't imagine him getting wound up and tense, the way Tate was almost all of the time, especially lately. I asked him about how he'd met Tate, and he told me how he'd come to the States on a college exchange program. They were in the same math class, always arguing with the professor about certain equations and their application. They discovered a love of nature and going to off-the-beaten track destinations.

"Has he changed much since then?" I asked him, as casually as I could. I didn't want to show that I was too interested in Tate.

"In some ways, yes, in others, no," Felix said. He had an interesting accent. His time in the US had taken care of that, presumably.

"He was always a little intense, you know, obsessive almost. But this health stuff and the adventure trips, that is new."

"Mmm..." I processed this new information.

"I was best man at his wedding. Him and Star fifteen years ago." He shook his head. "That was something! A beach wedding, beautiful summer's afternoon and all of us barefoot in the sand."

I was desperate to know more but I didn't want to ask. Fortunately, Felix felt like talking.

"I thought he was too young to get married, you know," he leaned towards me, dropping his voice as if he was scared anyone would hear. "I liked Star, but she was, you know, not like him. She had a restless, wandering energy. I didn't think it would last and it didn't."

I told him that I'd met her in LA and told him a bit about the weekend, without going into all the saucy details about what I got up to there, especially between the sheets with Tate.

"I love LA!" Felix exclaimed. "It's like living in a movie!"

I laughed. "I think that is what Star thinks too! She's waiting for the photographers to take her picture whenever she leaves the house. She doesn't go anywhere before she has looked at herself from twenty different angles to ensure she doesn't look too fat or too old or too poor."

"Too poor?"

"I know, but shabby chic is a very particular look there. You have to look like you don't care about money, but actually do have it."

"How do you do that?"

I explained to him like he was a very dim child. "You get designer ripped jeans, very expensive, couture white t-shirts, that are the purest cotton or silk or whatever. But plain."

I shook my head. "I know, it's nuts, Summer explained it to me before we went up there."

"Summer is a cool kid," Felix said and I agreed with him there.

We had some wine with our lunch and by the time I made it back to the office, I realized I might as well go home. There was no point pretending I was able to work.

Outside the building, Felix caught my arm.

"I want to ask you something."

"Okay?"

I thought he was going to ask me about where he could score drugs or which club he should go to, but then he said, "Can I take you out sometime? Maybe tomorrow night? On a date?"

I felt my face going red. He was being so serious, so German about everything. Like we were talking about a dental appointment not a romantic rendezvous.

"Uhm... I don't know," I said, to be honest. "Maybe I need to check with Tate?"

I liked hanging out with Felix but I was not attracted to him at all. I also didn't want to annoy Tate any more than I already might have done. I wanted to hold on to my job as long as possible.

Felix looked away, a bit embarrassed. "Actually, I asked him."

"If we could go out?"

He nodded.

"What did he say?"

"He thought you had a boyfriend. Do you?"

I wondered why Tate would think that. I'd never spoken about a guy in my life.

"Uhm... no," I said. "But Tate..." I didn't finish the sentence, I didn't quite know what to say.

"There is something between you?"

"No, no, of course not!" I protested a bit much, perhaps. "In any case, he's seeing someone. Jacqueline from legal?"

Felix shook his head as if he hadn't heard of her.

"Looks like a Miss Universe," I said rolling my eyes and he grinned.

"Of course," he said.

"But I wouldn't want him thinking that I... you know, flirted with you?" I was blushing again. It wasn't exactly a topic I was comfortable with.

"Look, I'm only here another three nights and he is busy at the moment. It would be nice to do some fun things. I'm not talking marriage or anything." He winked at me, "Not yet..."

I felt my cheeks becoming even redder.

"Why not?" I said. "What do you feel like doing?"

"Let me surprise you," he said, lifting my hand to his lips and kissing it.

"I'll pick you up tomorrow evening?"

I nodded.

Then he winked at me again and sauntered off.

I knew I had to tell Tate about this. But what should I say? I didn't want him to think I liked Felix like that, but on the other hand maybe it would make him a little jealous to know others were interested in me even if he wasn't. Was this a dangerous game to play? Probably. But I had a feeling that I was already in the game and this was simply my next move.

I texted him: Felix asked me to come out tomorrow night. That ok?

He responded a few minutes later with a thumbs up emoji.

What was that all about?

Chapter 16

Tate

I've made dinner, put out plates and call Summer to come down.

She stops as soon as she reaches the table.

"What is that?" she asks suspiciously.

"Lasagna, I think" I say, innocently.

"Made of...?" she puts her hands on her hips.

"Oh, come on!" I say. "Just have a bite!"

She doesn't move an inch. "Is it vegetarian?"

I nod and only tell her about the lentils to get her to sit down.

She pulls a face like I've told her the pasta had been mixed with lama droppings.

"And cheese?"

"This is a great new vegan cheese..." I start.

"Yuck, Dad!" She pushes her plate away.

"Just one bite," I coax her. I know children can't stand healthy food but I want to expose her at least to this kind of thinking. Maybe later in life, she'll remember something her old man said about looking after your body.

She takes a bite and then concedes, "It's all right. Can I have ice cream now?"

"Ice cream?" I hadn't put that on the shopping list.

"Evie brought some the other day," Summer says with a naughty grin. "I hid it in the fridge behind the frozen berries."

I scowl. Evie, Evie, Evie. Even when I'm alone with Summer, I can't get away from the girl.

Felix comes down the stairs, smelling like a male perfume counter.

"Ok, guys, I'm off. Wish me luck!"

I'd come home early, thinking Felix and I could catch a few waves and some beers after, but he informed me he was heading out on a date. With Evie. I'd warmed up lasagna for us, but Felix had a better idea.

"What's wrong, Dad?" Irritation must have been all over my face.

"I bit into something," I say quickly.

"You're not mad that Felix is off with Evie?" she asked. So perceptive.

"Why would I?"

"You like her, don't you?" she teases me.

"Of course, I do, she's my PA," I say.

"Not like that! I mean like, like," says Summer. "And she likes you too."

I sigh. "It's not like that, Summer."

"But it could be," she says, looking expectantly at me.

"No," I say gently, "It couldn't."

I'm surprised that she likes Evie this much. I can't recall Summer ever having approved of any of the women in my life. Usually she only has harsh words for the women I have dated. I recall the only serious relationship I'd had after the divorce. It was with a designer called Olga. A lovely woman who was also divorced but without children. Our relationship was wonderful, she had her flat and I had my house. We usually spent weekends together, but didn't see each other in the week. It worked well for both of us as we each had busy careers.

But Summer hated her, properly loathed her.

No matter what I did, she went out of her way to be mean and rude to Olga, hiding her clothes, spilling wine on her at dinner, refusing to come out of her room when Olga was there. I tried reasoning with Summer but she wouldn't budge and in the end, it meant the end of the relationship.

"Don't you want me to be happy?" I'd asked her, exasperated one night.

"What about my happiness?" she'd countered and had, of course, won that round.

But for some reason, she'd taken to Evie, even calling her a friend. I remembered the therapist who'd told me years ago that Summer had trust issues, and felt a deep sense of abandonment by her mother. I couldn't let Evie go if she was that important to Summer. Keeping my daughter grounded and stable was a priority to me. She'd not known about LA, as far as I could tell, about what had happened between Evie and me. I was going to keep it that way.

"A relationship would only mess things up," I said, as honest as I could be with her.

"Evie and I get on really well. Sometimes that is better than a relationship."

Summer nodded and I wished that I could believe my own words.

Instead, I was constantly wondering what Evie and Felix were getting up to.

Were they drinking? Dancing? Had Felix tried to kiss her yet? I knew he would.

Earlier, when I had spoken to him, I'd asked him about his girlfriend Janina.

"Oh, we broke up," he said casually.

They'd been together for years and years. Practically married. I knew she was bossy, a bit bitchy, on the occasions where I had met her she had been very cool towards me. When I asked him about it, he laughed it off, saying she was that way with everyone.

"What happened?" I asked.

We were standing outside on the veranda, looking at the sea. Felix did not seem particularly upset about the break-up, which he said, happened over a year ago.

"You never said anything?" I said.

He shrugged. "Things were bad for a long time. She had the dog remember?"

I did recall him telling me how she had kept the dog that gave him terrible allergies, insisting that it was not the dog's fault that he was allergic to it. It meant they had to have separate apartments and the dog was always getting in the way of their social calendar. They couldn't go away for the weekend, because who would look after Bruno? And he had a special diet and routine and needed his walks along a certain route or else he would become depressed or something.

It was insane.

Felix put up with all of it though because he felt sorry for Janina. Or so he thought. He found out one night that the tattoo on her arm, of a big thundercloud, was not about how she loved stormy weather, but to pay tribute to a friend of hers, Storm, a man she had not told Felix she had been romantically involved with. Every time he saw the tattoo now, he kept wondering what else she hadn't told him about. He couldn't get past it.

I got it.

Sometimes the little things were worse than the big things.

"You and Star?"

"It's okay," I told him, telling him a little about LA. "She is serious about this Trevor guy, maybe he can give her what she needs."

"And what is that? Prescription meds for schizophrenia?"

I looked at him and he quickly apologized. "Sorry, I've gone off crazy chicks."

"You think Star is crazy?"

"You don't?"

"Maybe a little," I conceded.

To me, a certain kind of insanity went hand in hand with creative thinking and passion and enthusiasm. I liked a certain kind of lawlessness, but even I believed in following some of the rules. Especially in my old age.

I told myself to let Felix and Evie have fun.

If she slept with him, it would be fine, it would be a sign that she'd moved on, that we could go back to being friends at work. And she could stay in Summer's life. I really wanted that to be true.

But I kept listening for Felix's car.

By midnight, I went to bed, taking a sleeping tablet.

I needed my sleep and I was not going to lie awake all night wondering if Felix was staying over at Evie's place.

I had very strange dreams that night.

All about men in boats, with semi-automatic rifles, dark glasses and receding hairlines. A little like a Godfather movie, but set in modern times, here in San Francisco. We were at my father's yacht down by the harbor and someone wanted to kill me, I jumped in the water and nearly drowned but at the last moment, a huge wave washed me to the jetty. It didn't exactly make sense.

When I got up the next morning, Felix's car was not outside.

He must have spent the night elsewhere.

I decided to go for a swim, without the wet suit, to wake me up properly.

The water was cold and I felt the shock of it straight away, reveling in it. It took my body a few minutes to warm up, then I no longer felt the cold or anything else. My anger, my worry, all the things that had been weighing down on me, lifted away and drifted off. I started swimming in the open water, out to the open sea, turning around only when my watch said I'd been out twenty minutes. I didn't want to get too cold. By the time I was back on the sand, shivery, my teeth clattering, all I could think about was coffee and a hot shower.

Nothing else mattered.

When I came down from the shower, the nanny was already there, getting Summer's things ready for school.

"Good morning," she said to me.

"It certainly is!" I said with a big smile. The endorphins had kicked in from my swim and I was feeling on top of the world.

Chapter 17

E^{vie} I guess I wanted to make him a little jealous.

That's not a crime is it?

To show him that other men were interested in me, appreciated me and wanted to be nice to me? He'd been so cold and distant towards me since LA, not even referring to it. It was as if it hadn't happened, none of it. I couldn't quite understand how he could be so disconnected from me and what had happened between us.

When Felix called me the next day while I was at work, I turned my back to Tate's office to take the call. The door was open and in my computer screen, I noticed him glancing my way, so I knew he was listening.

"Hey there," I said, more warmly than I would have if he wasn't listening.

"I'm sorry about last night," Felix said, sounding apologetic. He'd passed out on my couch at the flat I shared with Luisa. He'd had too much to drink and I didn't think he should drive. He'd fallen asleep right away and when I left for work in the morning, he was still out for the count. Luisa had already left for class so I left him to wake up in his own time.

"I don't know what came over me," he said.

I knew what had come over him, the wine at dinner, followed by shooters at the club. I had paced myself, but he had really put the drinks away.

"I was just having such a good time," he said miserably.

"Me too," I said with feeling. I checked in the screen, Tate was watching me.

"It was a wonderful evening," I said, then got up and left our office, supposedly to get some privacy. My point was made.

"Was it?" Felix said.

I laughed. Now that I was out of earshot, I no longer needed to pretend.

"It's okay, you had too much to drink! It happens! Especially when you haven't eaten dinner!"

"Oh, that's right," he said weakly. "I forgot, we went straight for drinks."

"You said we could eat later, but then... you wanted to dance!"

"I wanted to dance," he mumbled.

He sounded so pitiful, I felt sorry for him. He'd told me during the earlier part of the evening, before he had gotten so incredibly wasted, that he'd been wanting to have some fun for a while. Work had been dreary and the weather in Germany was horrible. It was supposed to have been summer, but it had been cold and rainy for weeks and now winter was coming. He had grabbed at the opportunity to come to California, even though he didn't need to be there in person.

The fact that he had finally broken up with his partner of many years was another reason for celebration. He told me that he had tried to break up with Janina many times but each time she threatened to jump off a bridge or harm herself in some dramatic way and he ended up staying, even though he wasn't happy with her anymore.

Now that he'd finally gotten free of her, he'd wanted to celebrate and had overdone it.

"Let me make it up to you," Felix said. "Can I take you out again tonight?"

I didn't want to give him the wrong idea. Felix was a lovely guy but only a friend.

"No drinking," I said. "Just dinner?"

"No drinking, absolutely," he said, sounding relieved.

"It will have to be an early night, ok? I have a lot of work in the morning," I said.

As soon as I ended the call, I went back to my desk.

Tate office door was closed. He was on a call with some industry big wig and in a few hours, he had a workshop with a client. I carried on preparing for that workshop, putting together the agenda, adding the talking points like he'd asked me to.

After five I got up and stood outside his office, waving goodbye. He looked at me and nodded, but I could see he was deep in conversation with the other person.

I got on the bus, thought about the evening ahead, not really in the mood for meeting Felix.

I thought about getting out of the date for the evening. He was much too keen and I wasn't interested in him. I took out my phone, about to text him to cancel our night out when a message from Tate came in: Need my laptop. Left it at home. Please get it. Need it for the workshop!

Shit.

I was almost at home. I'd have to get an Uber to drive me over to his house and this time of the day, traffic would be a nightmare.

I answered: Will get it now. Leaving from home.

I got a car right away but as I'd feared, the roads were jam-packed. The workshop would start in an hour and he probably could get going without the laptop, but I knew there were important slides on it that he wanted to show. But I could email them to him from the house once I was there.

I got there after six, running up the stairs to Tate's study at the top of the house.

"What's going on?" Summer came in and I quickly explained to her that I needed her father's laptop. She helped me look for it but we couldn't find it.

"Maybe he left it in his bedroom? Sometimes he works in bed?" Summer said and we went into his room, but it wasn't there either.

The workshop would already have gotten underway.

"What about downstairs?" I asked, growing increasingly panicky. We ran down the stairs, started looking in the kitchen and lounge but the housekeeper had already cleaned up everything there.

"Evie?" Felix came up through the open doors. He had his jeans rolled up for a walk on the beach.

I held up a hand, to show him I was in the middle of something and couldn't talk.

I heard Summer whisper to him, "She's looking for Dad's laptop."

I took out my phone, quickly texted Tate: Laptop not here. Looked all over.

He responded a few minutes later: In car maybe?

I stared at the screen.

"What did he say?" Summer asked. I told her.

"Is he at the office? Then he can get it, right?" Felix said.

I shook my head. "He's stuck in that meeting. I'll have to go back there."

"But surely he can just pop out?"

"No..." I said.

"Take my car," Felix said. "It will be faster."

There was no time to argue. He walked out with me to his rental car. "This is not like Tate. He always knows where his laptop is."

He was right, something felt off.

"Maybe he knows exactly where it is and is just enjoying ordering you around?"

"Don't be ridiculous!" I snapped at him and jumped into the car. But I thought about what he said as I drove back to the city, as fast as I could. There was hardly any traffic heading back but once I was in the heart of city center, it was slow-moving again.

Would Tate do that? Send me out on a fool's errand, knowing full well where the laptop was.

Of course he would, I thought. Especially after than stunt I'd pulled with the phone call earlier, wanting to make him jealous. This was his way of punishing me.

By the time I got to the car park, I already knew I wouldn't find the laptop in his car. A little while later, his message came: Found it! All good.

I didn't respond.

I simply got back into Felix's car and drove it back, again, to Tate's house.

When I got there, I marched into the house and found Felix sitting outside, having a beer.

"Did you get it?"

I shook my head, too angry to talk.

"I'm sorry, I'm not up to going out tonight," I said. He nodded, I could see he was trying to be understanding. "It's been too long a day and I just want to go home."

"Of course, let's have a drink while you wait for the Uber?

I agreed.

The sun was beginning to set but it was overcast and so there wasn't much of a sunset. It hadn't been much of a day either. "I opened a bottle of wine," said Felix, handing me a glass. "It's a good wine, but I think Tate won't mind, he owes you."

I was trying to get a car, but sitting down with a glass of wine in my hand, I suddenly didn't feel like rushing off.

"It's my fault," I said, with a sigh. "I think he was trying to punish me."

Felix frowned. "Why?"

"He heard me talking on the phone to you earlier."

"So? He said he was okay with us seeing each other."

"I don't think he is, though."

I finished my glass and had another. So much for not wanting to have a big night. But it felt good sitting with Felix, talking about Tate and how tense our relationship had become. "This does not sound healthy," Felix said.

Inside, Annika was warming up dinner for Summer.

"I should get going," I said, making no move to get up though. The sun had gone down but we had some warm blankets to pull over us. Felix told me about his meetings, which he thought had gone well enough but would probably not result in the kind of deal the Americans wanted. "We tend to do things differently in Germany. We're more careful, risk averse."

But he didn't want to go back. "I like it here," he said, giving me a frank, direct stare. His hand was close to my arm and he lifted a finger, stroking my arm very gently. A little current of electricity ran up my skin. I knew what he was telling me and I what I should tell him, but for the first time that day, I was relaxing and I was enjoying myself.

At that moment, the front door opened, and Tate walked in. He saw us sitting outside and came out. "Well, well, well," he said with a strange little smile. "This does look cozy."

Chapter 18

T ate

As soon as I came out onto the patio, Felix moved away from Evie, who was not looking at me. Her mouth was set in a thin line. She was angry with me, had figured out what I was up to, obviously.

"Can I get you some wine?" Felix asked and went in to get a glass.

"About earlier," I said breezily. "Sorry for all the runaround, turns out I had the bloody laptop all along."

"Bullshit," Evie said in an even tone, but there was anger simmering underneath. "You knew you had it, you just liked the idea of making me sweat."

"You're right there," I said, liking the direction this conversation was going.

"I've had enough though," she said, finally looking me in the eye. "I'm quitting, you can play your games with someone else now."

I considered her for a moment, wondered what kind of play this was.

Felix came out with the wine and I raised the glass. "To your last night." Felix fetched his glass, touched mine. "Looks like you had a good visit. A very good visit, indeed," I nodded in Evie's direction, making it clear what I meant.

Felix looked down, uncomfortable, unsure what to say.

Evie got up. "You know what, I'm going home." She leaned to kiss Felix's cheek. "It was lovely to meet you by the way, good luck for everything back home." Then she looked me in the eye and said, "As for you, fuck you." She walked past me, into the house, saying something to Summer.

"Tate, what is going on?!" Felix touched my arm but I shook it off.

"Is there something going on between you and Evie?"

"What do you think?" I snapped at him. He stood back, thrown by my aggressive response. Felix was always so mild-mannered, so decent. So bloody boring. I wished he would fuck off.

I went in after Evie.

This was not going as planned.

"Dad?" Summer looked at me as I came into the house. She was doing her homework at the kitchen counter.

"Hey, sweetheart," I tried to smile at her.

"Everything okay?" she asked.

"Sure."

"Where's Evie?"

"I think she's gone home."

I went out the front door, saw her walk down to the beach. I followed her.

"Evie, wait," I called to her.

But she didn't turn around.

I picked up the pace, but she did too, going down the side of the house, down to the beach.

"Evie, wait up!" I called to her.

She flew around, furious. "Oh, now you want to talk. Now you're ready to treat me like a human being, when it suits you!"

I was surprised by her anger, the intensity I had not seen before. She was usually so composed. It was cold and dark out on the beach. The sound of the waves crashing onto the sand was loud, I had to raise my voice to make myself heard.

"I'm sorry, okay!" I called out to her.

She stopped walking.

I sighed, the game was up, it was time to play it straight.

"I took things too far," I admitted.

"You admit that you chased me around today just to mess with me?"

I nodded. "Yes."

"That is seriously fucked up," she said.

"Yeah well, you wanted me to think you and Felix had hooked up, right? Not exactly mature either?"

She knew I was right, I could see it in the way her body relaxed, the shoulders untensing.

"Why have you been so distant to me? Since LA?" She asked.

I'm not good at these kinds of conversations, avoiding them at all costs. But I was losing Evie, and I didn't want that to happen. That meant, doing this, having this talk.

"Look, that's just me. I'm not good at relationships."

"We don't have a relationship," Evie said. "We slept together, twice."

"In my books, that is a long term relationship," I chuckled but she turned away.

"Look, I have feelings for you and I don't like it," I admitted. "I hoped if I pulled away a bit, the feelings would go too. But it hasn't happened. And when you talked to Felix like that, I don't know, it's like I went crazy. I couldn't handle seeing you with him." Then I admitted, "I couldn't handle the thought of us, together, but that was somehow worse. You with someone else."

The sound of a dog, barking loudly, came towards us. It was unclear where the dog was. She gave a step back and bumped into me.

I didn't move away and she didn't either. She stood with her back against my chest and I reached out and put my arms around her. She didn't move, she didn't say a word, but then leaned back her head ever so slightly.

"Evie," I murmured, burying my face in her hair, finding her neck, kissing it.

My hands slipped underneath the top she was wearing, moving up to her breasts, cupping them in my hands and squeezing them. I let my right hand slide down her belly and into her jeans, under the waistband, into her panties. I heard her gasp as my fingers reached lower. Her breathing was becoming louder but she didn't push me away. I reached lower over her pubic bone, feeling between her legs and finding her clitoris, pulsating and quivering and started rubbing it rhythmically, slowly. For a few moments, she let me touch her, feel her, my desire building and then she pulled away from me.

"No," she said, her breathing ragged.

She fumbled with her clothes, straightening everything.

"This has got to stop."

"You don't want it to stop," I said.

"No," she said. "I don't, but that is part of the problem isn't it?"

"What do you mean?"

She shook her head. "What we're doing, it's not... healthy."

"But I want you," I said, pulling her back to me and kissing her. She kissed me back, her tongue finding mine and twisting around it, going deeper and deeper. I was in delicious agony.

She pulled away again, but this time not as firmly as before.

"We're not children. We don't just want things and take them without considering our actions."

"I do," I said, pulling her against me. "I go for what I want, and right now, that's you."

I kissed her again and we slid down onto the sand.

The roar of the ocean in the background was loud, but I didn't hear it. I was aware only of the pounding of my blood in my ears, the excitement building as we kissed passionately, clinging at each other. I pushed her down onto the sand and slid on top of her. The heat was intense. Where moments before I had been aware of the cold, I now only felt the energy between us, the warmth of her skin. There was an urgency to our movements, I had the sense she was slipping away from me and I wanted to hold on to her, to find her. I entered her, felt her opening up to me, warm, wet and welcoming and I couldn't have stopped myself even if I'd wanted to.

There was the muffled ping of a notification from her phone bringing us back to reality.

Evie gasped, "That's my car."

She pulled away, buttoning her jeans up, pulling her top back on and running up to the road. She was running away from me again, and I went after her.

"Evie!" I called but she didn't turn around again.

It was as if she couldn't wait to get away from me.

I got up slowly and went out into the road, but the car had long gone. Then I walked up to the house, but lingered a while. I was in no rush to face Summer or Felix, I wanted to savor what had just happened. The sheer ecstasy of our coupling was intoxicating, I'd never had this kind of intensity in a relationship before. It was almost animal, this physical joining of our bodies, the way we connected, our movements in perfect harmony, the most physical of dances.

I knew Evie felt it too, no matter what she said, the way she responded to me, showed that she felt it too.

When I got back to the house, Summer had gone from the kitchen, probably to watch television. I went outside, but Felix had gone too.

I knocked on his door and went in.

I found him packing his bag.

"You don't need to go," I said.

He nodded but carried on packing, his face tight and closed off.

"I'm sorry about all that," I said, meaning my behavior, the way I'd acted.

Again, he said nothing.

But he took his jacket, then his bag and said to me, "You should have told me the truth. We've known each other for what, fifteen years? You couldn't be honest?"

Ah, man, the Germans where so correct. Even Felix, it seemed, had a rule book for friendships.

"Listen, Felix..."

"No," Felix shook his head. "I thought we were friends. Maybe we were once, but we've moved on, right? That happens."

"No," I said, trying to fix what was coming undone right in front of my eyes.

"Wait, Felix! We are friends, come on, you can't think that this...what happened... changed any of that?"

He looked at me, a strange mix of pity and dislike in his eyes. "You have changed," he said, softly.

"You are not who you used to be."

"Of course not!" I called out. "I've grown up, we all have. But we are still friends!"

"No," Felix said carefully. "Not anymore."

Then he walked out the door and down the stairs. I should have gone after him but his words had a curious effect on me, paralyzing me. I didn't want to face him again, continue this conversation. If he wanted to go like this, it was fine by me. He'd hardly been blameless in the whole affair. Typical of him not to want to take any responsibility for his actions. He knew the kind of pressure I was under.

I went to take a shower and thought about Evie, how good it felt to feel her skin against me again.

Chapter 19

Evie

"Aren't you going to work?" Luisa asks me the next morning, when I come out of my room after nine, still dressed in my pajamas.

"Nope," I say.

She frowns, looks at me suspiciously. "You don't look sick?"

"I'm not," I say and then give a big grin. "I just quit."

She stares at me. "Why?"

"Long story," I say, not keen to get into it now. "Not a good fit? Isn't that what the HR people always say?"

Luisa looks at me like I'm going insane. Maybe I am. I'm certainly acting out of character. But then she grabs her things, "What are you doing today?"

"No plans," I say and she asks if I can do her a favor. She was supposed to do the shopping for her granny but she has a busy day and could I help her out?

"Of course," I say.

"You're an angel!" Relief spreads across Luisa's face, but then she becomes serious again.

"I'll text you the list. It's not a lot, but she gets certain things from certain shops, like the chorizo from the deli. I'll share the location with you. Don't try to get it from Costco, ok? She'll know and give you hell!"

I can't help but smile at the thought of such a difficult old lady.

Soon after Luisa left, I got a call from Jill from HumanITy.

"I received your email," she said in a formal voice. "May I enquire your reasons for leaving?"

"I'd rather not talk about it," I say.

"Oh," she says, surprised by my response. "Your contract has specifications about a termination. You need to give a month's notice, at least."

If she was trying to intimidate me, it wasn't working.

I wasn't the same impressionable girl I had been only three months ago.

I took a breath. "It's better this way, you can check with Tate, Mr. Sagarro, I mean."

There is a pause on the line. "Did something happen, Evie? You can tell me."

"As I say, I'd prefer not to discuss this," I say. "If there is nothing else, I need to go, I have someplace I need to be."

Then I put down the phone and took a bus to the Latino side of town, spending a pleasant couple of hours going to the fruit seller on one street corner for mangoes, then right across town to a deli in a backstreet for a particular kind of cheese. I arrived at Luisa's grandmother's place at around lunchtime. She was staying in a kind of subsidized senior citizen community with separate apartments. I pressed the buzzer for her place and was let inside. At her door, I knocked again.

"Who is it?" She called from inside.

"Mrs. Gomez? My name is Evie, I'm your granddaughter Luisa's roommate."

"Says who?" The old lady's voice came from inside, suspicious. "You could be coming here to steal my money, hit me over the head and run off to go get drugs."

I had to laugh. "Luisa told me to tell Miguel that the chorizo he sold you last time was too fatty, and he gave me a special price on this one."

The door opened a tiny bit and a wrinkly face appeared in the gap.

"You live with Luisa?" The old lady asked.

"Yes, she asked me to help her out today. She has a test later on and I, well, I quit my job and was at a loose end."

"Why you quit your job?" she fired back at me.

I laughed. "Well, it got complicated with my boss."

"Why? He come on to you?"

I had nothing to lose by telling the truth. "We slept together and then he treated me like shit."

The door closed and opened properly. Luisa's grandmother stood in front of me, almost a head smaller than me, a face lined and wrinkled but with brown eyes as sharp and alive as they must have been sixty years ago.

"I'll put the kettle on," she said, leaving the door open for me to come in.

The small apartment was filled with clutter, a mess of newspapers and magazines. I knew from Luisa that her grandmother had been living in the apartment for the past ten years. There were aides supposed to assist the seniors in the complex but they were in high demand and there was often no one to help Mrs. Gomez with her shopping. The arthritis in her knees made walking and carrying heavy bags a problem. While I helped unpack her shopping and cleaned the kitchen for her, she listened to my sorry tale, making clicking noises with her tongue to indicate her disapproval.

"You need a nice boy, someone like my grandson Filippo. He's got his own auto shop."

I shook my head. "No, I think I'm done with men for a while."

She gave me a sharp look. "You want him to beg you to take him back?"

"He won't do that," I said.

I'd told her that Tate Sagarro was not the type who begged or asked. He took what he wanted. He was used to getting his own way.

"But you are playing hard ball," the old lady said, slapping the table hard, and cackling like an old witch. "I like that!"

I didn't want to tell her that no, I wasn't playing any game anymore. I felt like I had let him use me, given in to desire even though I knew it wasn't what I wanted. I had feelings for Tate, I wanted to be with him. The job had always been about him, I didn't care about the actual work at all. The money had been good but it wasn't enough. I didn't want to be treated the way he had been treating me, blowing hot and cold, depending on his mood. And it was humiliating, the way he had sent me running all over town that afternoon, looking for a laptop that he had with him the whole time. It was controlling and arrogant and I didn't want to be at the mercy of that kind of man. I could hardly believe this was the same man who had been so nice to me in Los Angeles, showing me the Sunset Strip and taking me for ice cream all over the city.

But then he changed. Again. And I'd had enough. I couldn't do this anymore.

I saw that he'd called me and I'd ignored his calls all day.

Felix had called me earlier from the airport and I took his call.

"I wanted to thank you for going out with me the other night," he said. "That was probably the highlight of my trip."

"What a shitty time you must've had!" I said with a laugh.

"It wasn't the best trip ever," he admitted wryly. Then he said, "Actually, Tate and I had an argument before I left." He told me about the words that had been exchanged and how he felt their friendship had suffered a fatal blow.

"But you know, I was thinking this morning, Tate never wanted to get married. He told me years ago that he preferred to be alone, that he found people too noisy."

"Noisy?"

"Ja, I always thought that was a strange word to use. But I think he meant, people make demands, they interfere with his life, they intrude in his thinking. He doesn't know how to deal with people."

"He deals with Summer just fine."

"Does he, really?" Felix asked me. "Don't you find he doesn't really talk to her, he lets her do whatever she wants. But how much time do they spend together? I think that is why she liked you so much. You watched TV with her, did stuff with her."

"You mean, I let her eat ice cream and junk food."

"You let her be a kid."

And I let Tate be a man, I thought. I let him be a sexual being. But there was more to life and I wanted more from life. I wanted someone to treat me well, to talk to me, to trust me. The kind of relationship my parents had, where even if people weren't the same, when they did get together, it was good. You could see from a mile away that my parents loved each other. It was in the way my mother rested a hand on my father's shoulder at the dinner table, the way my dad brought her coffee in bed in the morning.

It was in the small things.

I wanted small things, not big gestures or romantic experiences.

I spent the rest of the day at Mrs. Gomez's place, helping her tidy the place, water the ferns, move a chair that was in the way. We did some laundry and then I helped her neighbor, Mrs. Cabrera to do her laundry. There was a communal washing line and I hung up the elasticated pants and faded bed linen.

"I'll come back tomorrow," I promised, "Help you take it down."

"You could get a job here any day, you know," Mrs. Cabrera said. "They pay peanuts but it's better than nothing."

"I happen to like peanuts," I said but she waved a hand, "Give me terrible gas, nuts do."

I had to laugh again.

But spending time with the old ladies had cheered me up.

Mrs. Gomez told me about her years on a Californian avocado farm, where she had spent most of her adult life, until her husband had managed to get his Green Card. They moved to the city, sent their kids to school, and she watched her sons get married and her daughters get divorced.

"You young people, you expect too much of the men," she said.

"We do?"

"Oh yes," she nodded sagely. "Men are like goats. Stubborn, dumb. But you need them around. What is a home without a goat?"

I smiled all the way home. I had never had much to do with goats. The little I knew of goats extended to them being smelly and rather dirty, not exactly the kind of creature you wanted to have around. But according to Mrs. Gomez, they were very handy creatures, and their milk made good cheese. You could even eat the meat when you fell on hard times. All this according to Mrs. Gomez, who said if she had to choose between having a goat and having a man, the goat would win every time.

Chapter 20

Tate

My phone rings as I'm driving in to work a bit late, feeling great after an early morning surf.

My good mood vanishes quickly though.

It's Jill and she kicks off the call with, "Evie Gerick has resigned. Did you know about this?"

"What?"

I did not see that coming.

An image flashes into my mind of the two of us on the beach last night.

"Tate! What did you do?!"

I snap out of my reverie. "What do you mean?"

Jill is talking to me like I'm a naughty child and she's caught me out in a lie.

"You know what I'm talking about!"

"I don't!"

"This is the second PA to resign in under three months in less than a year! Clearly, something happened."

I wonder if having mind blowing sex would count as "something happening" in Jill's world, I think to myself with a smile.

"I'm sure it's not real," I say, refusing to believe it.

"Oh, it's real!" she snaps. "I called to discuss it with her and she wouldn't talk about it. She said to talk to you if I wanted more details."

"Really?"

"Jesus, Tate!" Jill sounded upset. "Will you come down to Earth sometime?!"

"What are you talking about? You sound a little stressed, Jill, do you need a break perhaps?"

Jill was probably counting to ten or something, because the line was very quiet.

"I'll see you at the office later," she said in a flat voice, ending the call.

I was chuckling to myself, having rather enjoyed that interaction. But after a few minutes, the thrill wore off. I started thinking of the implications of what she'd told me. Evie resigning like that meant that our interlude on the beach had not changed her mind at all. She'd told me she was quitting at the house. But I thought she was bluffing, trying to get attention. The fact that she had resigned this morning put a whole different light on things.

I called her but she didn't pick up.

She'd been working on the presentation for my upcoming UK trip. I needed that. Would she have left it on her computer at work? There were other things I'd relied on Evie to do for me, I didn't know what they were off hand, that's why I had her; she'd been taking care of it. There was someone I needed to call today, who was it again?

My good mood was entirely gone by the time I reached work.

I flew into the office, switched Evie's computer on and started searching through her files and emails. I couldn't find the presentation anywhere. Where the hell was it?

I called her again.

I sent messages.

Nothing.

Then Tim Henley from the London office called and I was pulled into a strategy meeting that lasted the rest of the morning. I kept sneaking peeks at my phone but she didn't call me back or text me back.

By the time I was finished with the meeting, I was famished. What was I having for lunch? Usually Evie sorted something out but nothing had been delivered and there was nobody booked in my diary. Lunch was the most important meal of my day, it was basically my only meal as I started my fast shortly after that. I'd not had breakfast this morning and was feeling a bit crabby. I opened the fridge in the office kitchen and saw a nice-looking salad.

"I hope you're not thinking of eating that," someone said behind me.

I turned to find one of the young interns looking at me. Recognizing me, she blushed, "Oh, I'm sorry Mr. Sagarro, please have my lunch."

Jesus, as if I was going to start eating my employees' lunch!

I walked out of the kitchen and decided to pop over to my favorite sushi bar.

I tried calling Evie again but she didn't answer.

I didn't even know where she lived.

How was that possible?

I called the office and asked to be put through to one of the HR staff, but not Jill. I didn't want her knowing that I wanted Evie's home address. I could only imagine to what conclusions she might jump. She wouldn't be wrong, of course, but that had nothing to do with it. I told someone that I wanted to send Evie flowers as she was having a personal crisis.

"Can I take care of that for you, Sir?" the HR lady asked.

"Ah, no. I want to do it myself," I said.

"O-kay," she said, and I could hear she thought it strange. I was obviously not the kind of boss who took flowers to employees' houses. But she gave me the address and as soon as I'd eaten enough, I headed over to Evie's place. It was in the student part of town, lots of boxy apartments jumbled together on crowded streets. So many young people, I almost forgot what it was like to be that young, barely out of diapers but ready to conquer the world.

I found her apartment and got in easily enough.

It was an ugly apartment building with dirty walls and stained floors. Good Lord, Evie lived here? There was no elevator, only a staircase that smelled of beer and urine. I slowed down my pace, careful not to put my designer sneakers into anything disgusting. I'd probably throw them away later anyway.

I knocked on her door.

A buxom Latina girl opened the door.

"Yes?"

"I'm looking for Evie?"

"Why?" she stared me down. I liked the attitude.

"I'm her boss," I said.

"You mean, you were her boss."

Ouch.

"Is she here?"

"Nope," the girl said, still standing in the doorway.

"Do you want to leave a message?"

I looked at her and considered my options. I had a feeling she knew a lot of what was going on, perhaps more than I did. I knew people didn't give me credit for being too clued up when it came to other people and their feelings, but I was a pretty good reader of people and this girl could help me.

"Can I come in?" I asked, giving her one of my most charming smiles.

Her eyes narrowed, but she opened the door and stepped back.

Inside, the place was small and grubby. Laundry hung on a rack by the window to dry. The couch was ratty, with a throw over the back and some faded cushions trying for some character against the back. There were books and paper everywhere, I was guessing the roommate was a student.

"Okay, so what do you want?" the girl crossed her arms and looked at me like I was trying to sell her car insurance even though she didn't have a car.

"You're friends with Evie," I stated. "You care about her."

She looked at me consideringly.

"So do I."

She laughed, rather loudly. "Bullshit. You just care about yourself, man."

"Why do you say that?"

"She's been working her ass off for you for months now. And do you ever say a thank you? Do you give her a bonus, a weekend off? No way. She's working weekends, driving your friends to the airport? Taking your daughter for ice cream?" She snorted and shook her head.

"She likes Summer," I said.

"Nobody likes their bosses daughter that much," she said, staring me down. "You've treated her like shit," she said.

"She told you that?"

"A blind person could see it," she said.

I wondered how much Evie had told her about what had happened between us. I had a feeling this girl knew more than I'd want her too.

"Look, I don't know what you know…"

She interrupted me, "You know, Mr. Smooth-talking Genius, Silicon Valley Super Dick, what's-its-face? I don't give a shit what you have to say. Why don't you take your moneyed ass out of here and go fuck up some other young girl's life. Because you've got a real gift for it, Mister!"

Wow.

It had been a while since anyone had talked to me like that.

I was still coming up with a response when she put a hand on my chest and pushed me out of the apartment.

"I don't want to see you around here again. Next time, I'm calling the cops," she said, and slammed the door in my face.

I wanted to say something, to win her over, to convince her to help me find Evie, but it was clear that this was not going to happen anytime soon. This girl had me pegged as a bastard of the highest order, a real arsehole, the kind of man nobody wanted in their friend's life.

Oddly enough, I cared.

I never would have bothered with people like that before. If someone didn't like me, I shrugged them off and moved on. But this girl's opinion mattered. Because Evie mattered. That much was clear to me. I cared what she thought of me and until a few hours ago, I thought she'd really liked me, physically as well as otherwise. I mean, what else was there but physical connection? In my book, chemistry was more important than personality, than income, perhaps even intellect. When it came to women, I didn't want to talk math and science, I wanted to talk dirty and have sex. Good sex. Great sex. All of which I had with Evie. I'd been serious when I told Evie that I thought of us as having a relationship.

I knew other people thought relationships were about watching TV together, eating pizza on couches, gossiping about friends and family members. But I wasn't like that. I didn't want any of that. I thought Evie didn't either.

Perhaps I was wrong.

That evening, watching Summer pick her way through a dinner of noodles and chicken, I asked her,

"Do you think I'm a nice guy?"

Summer looked up and blinked.

"A what?"

"A nice guy?"

She started laughing.

"What?"

"A nice guy?! Since when do you want to be a nice guy?"

"I'm not saying I want to be a nice guy, I'm wondering what people think of me."

"A cunt," I heard the nanny say behind me.

I swung around. "What?"

"Handsome, very clever, but essentially, yes, a cunt."

Perhaps that was how they referred to jocks in Sweden, I thought. But the look in her eyes seemed to suggest otherwise.

Summer was still laughing.

"What's going on, Dad?" she asked.

"Evie quit," I said.

She dropped her fork. "What?"

I hadn't thought about her reaction. But her eyes filled with tears and I could see she was about to cry. The nanny moved in to comfort her, then looked at me and mouthed the word "Cunt."

Later, when I was upstairs, working on my laptop, Summer came in to say goodnight.

Her eyes were rimmed red and swollen. "Get her back, Dad," she said. I got up and gave her a hug. I didn't need to ask who she was talking about.

I knew.

"I will, sweetheart. I will."

Chapter 21

E vie
    I am standing in the amusement park, feeling my heartrate quicken as the queue moves to the front of the line. Any minute I'll have to hand over my ticket and step into the little steel box, strap myself in and go hurling through the air.

Why am I doing this again?

I am going through the motions, but my heart is beating fast, then I look back and see Luisa standing at the back, in the crowd, holding out a thumbs up. I try to smile and wave back. My mouth is so dry.

This morning, in our apartment, Luisa asked me what I was doing that day and I said I was going to take Mrs. Fuentes to the hairdresser.

"Why?"

"She needs someone to take her," I said with a shrug.

"They have people there to help her, you know?" Luisa said incredulous.

"One of the care givers, Carl, is sick and she needs someone to take her because her vision is bad, she's got, like only ten percent sight, I think."

Luisa stared at me. "You have a business degree, girl! Can't you see you are seriously overqualified for this job?!"

"It's not like they're paying me," I mumbled. It had sounded like a good idea at the time, to help the old ladies at the senior center manage their life, but Luisa's reaction was making me wonder if maybe she was right.

"Look, I get it, they're nice, right? It's like being with your granny or something? But they are old people and you are young. You need to do young things, hang out with young people!" Luisa said.

I shrugged. The few friends I did have were working during the day.

"I've got the day off," said Luisa. "I was going to go do my nails, but let's do something together instead."

"Like what?"

She rolled her eyes. "Something young! Something fun!" Her eyes started twinkling. "Let's do something you've always been too scared to do."

Oh, my God. It sounded terrible. She was going to push me off a mountain or something. I really didn't feel like that. I thought of something Tate had said to me in LA, when I pretended to be his fiancé. We'd spent quite a lot of time together while having dinner with Trevor and Star, or waiting for Summer at the house. We'd talked, for once, not about work or apps or technology but about the things we liked and didn't like. Tate said he wasn't scared of anything, except boredom perhaps. I remembered thinking that I was scared of so many things, from heights to open water, wild animals to pitch black darkness. I told him about my fear of rollercoasters then and he'd shaken his head like he'd never heard of anything so absurd.

"We could ride a rollercoaster?" I said and Luisa clapped her hands. "Yes! Let's do that!" She wasn't scared of anything either, I thought, rather miserably as we headed out to the amusement park. She relished new challenges and adventures while I was always doubtful and suspicious. I called it careful, she said I was wimp.

It was Luisa who'd decided I should go alone on the rollercoaster.

She would wait for me on the ground. It was like she thought it I could conquer this fear, then I'd know what to do with my life and my future, I would be able to move on from Tate and the disastrous PA experience, somehow miraculously find my mission in life. I didn't know how to tell her that I was feeling more lost than ever. I had been the baby of my family all my life, protected by my brothers and parents, sheltered from all harmful situations and now I was too scared to do anything.

When it was my turn to get into the cubicle, my hands were shaking so much that the assistant had to buckle me up. "Are you okay?" He asked me. He looked about twelve years old, with angry acne that probably glowed in the dark.

I could only nod.

I tried not to think of the time when our family went to some festival when we were still living in Washington. My parents went off searching for food and my brothers were supposed to look after me. But then they'd gone off looking for their own entertainment. I was left to wander the fairground on my own. I was terrified, wandering from one noisy ride to another, freaked out by the shrieking children and the loud yelling. I couldn't tell if people were enjoying themselves or were terrified to death.

The rollercoaster started moving and I squeezed my eyelids shut. Behind me, I heard excited yelps of people anticipating the ride to come. I thought if I kept my eyes shut the whole time, I could maybe miss all of it.

Then I thought, no.

I didn't want to miss out on this. I was busy missing out on my whole life because I was scared. Of what, exactly? I'd read somewhere that I was more likely to be in a car accident than get hurt on a roller coaster. That was the whole point of this experience, you were completely safe in your harness, doing something very dangerous, yes, but you were safe. I opened my eyes carefully, felt the wind blow my hair back. The rollercoaster was teetering at the top of the track and I could feel it dipping down and then gathering speed. Behind me people were yelling and screaming at the top of their voices as the rollercoaster hurled about and threw us all over the place.

I couldn't see a thing, the world whipped past me in a blur but I felt the adrenaline rush through my blood. This was amazing! The rollercoaster climbed up again and I could see the track and the complicated structure that held us up. I couldn't imagine closing my eyes now. I would be missing out on so much, all of the excitement of the ride ahead.

The last part of the ride was the best, knowing what was coming and steeling myself for the incredible drop. Behind me one girl was shouting "Yes, yes, yes!" over and over again, it sounded like she was having an orgasm and this was so funny but I couldn't laugh. I was too distracted by what was happening to me to focus on it.

By the time the rollercoaster arrived back at the station, I was disappointed that the ride was over.

"How was it?" Luisa asked, rushing forward to meet me as I came off the ride.

"Was it scary? Did you freak out?"

It sounded like she was talking to a child. I felt like I was emerging from a tunnel into bright sunshine, there was a realization of what I had been missing out on in my life.

"No," I said, with a big smile. "It was fucking fantastic."

"There you go!" She gave me a high five and we went off looking for the next ride. I turned around to watch the next lot of people go on the ride and I almost felt envious of the experience they were about to have. This was the flagship ride of the amusement park, the highest and supposedly scariest of them all. But I'd done it, no problem, had even enjoyed it.

Luisa and I went on a few rides after that, ending the day with a session of go carts where we had loads of fun bumping our cars into each other and into the railing.

We headed back to our apartment in the afternoon, weary from all the excitement.

Luisa was supposed to go out with friends that night but she said she wanted to stay in.

"You've been very quiet," she said, looking at me. "You okay?"

I was thinking about a lot of things ever since that rollercoaster ride.

"I think you may have been right," I said.

"Yeah?" she was pleased.

I nodded. "I need to try new things, different things, figure out who I am."

"You don't know who you are?" Luisa asked, sarcastically.

I shook my head, slowly, "Not really, no."

She frowned.

"I thought I hated rollercoasters but as it turned out, I love them. I thought I wanted to work in the business world, but I didn't like it. I liked working for Tate, or really, seeing how he worked, how his mind worked. But all the email and the spreadsheets and the meetings? I don't like any of that."

"But you like the old people, right?" Luisa asked, knowingly.

"Yeah," I said. "I like working with people, helping people. That makes me feel good."

She nodded. "Makes sense. So what are you going to do now?"

I still didn't have an answer to that. But I knew I didn't want to go back to Lake Tahoe. I'd just slip into the role of becoming the baby of the family again, working in the hotel restaurant, making my way up into management, finally heading up the reception desk at the ski resort. It wasn't a bad life, but it wasn't what I wanted. I had enough money saved up for rent so I could afford to take more time to figure out what I wanted.

"Tomorrow, I will take Mrs. Fuentes for that haircut," I said.

"And after that?"

"I think maybe I'll go on a horse trail."

"What?" Luisa sat up.

"I've always been scared of horses. I don't know why. Maybe it's time to find out."

Luisa shook her head and laughed. "Girl, you're going off the rails, but in a good way. I like it!"

Later, I called Summer on her mobile phone.

"Evie!" I could hear the relief in her voice.

"Sorry I haven't called, I've been busy. Are you okay?"

"Yes! Sort of..." her voice fell. "Where are you?"

"I am still here, just not, at work," I said.

"I heard you left," she said, her voice becoming sad.

"I left work, not you," I said firmly.

"What does that mean?" her voice sounded small.

"We're still friends, if you want to be?"

"Yes, of course!" Summer sounded so relieved, it broke my heart.

"If you want, I can ask Annika to bring you for ice cream tomorrow afternoon? Or I could fetch you from school if you like, I just don't want Annika to get in trouble with your father." I decided to be as honest with Summer as I could be.

"Are you still mad at Dad?"

"Yes," I said. I couldn't have explained to Summer what I felt even if I'd wanted to. My feelings were too complicated and confusing. But they weren't good. And talking to Tate did not feel right, not now. Perhaps in the future, we could talk. But right now, he wanted to argue and spar and push me around with words. He was the master at all of the games.

I was only beginning to figure out which ones I liked to play.

Chapter 22

T ate

When I come back from London, I decide to go on a silent retreat at a place in the desert. I am hoping it will help give me a bit of clarity. Of course, it ends up giving me diarrhea instead. After two days at this weird, Native American sort of village, I start getting the runs and a bit of fever as well. I end up spending the days in my hut wondering if I'm supposed to sweat this much and feel this crap.

I'm guessing, yes.

People don't come on these sorts of things unless their lives have gone off in the wrong direction and they want to try and get back on track again. This is my understanding of it. No talking to anyone, no checking of phones, not that I could even if I wanted to. There is no signal here and so secretly surfing the web is impossible. This is the kind of place that I would normally never go to in a million years, but after London, I'm thinking it's worth a shot.

I'd nearly blown the entire deal.

After my first day, Tim Henley had invited me for a drink and came straight out and asked me what was going on.

"Nothing, why?"

We knew each other a little, Tim and I, so he felt he could talk to me.

"You're acting a little off, I have to tell you. The guys have told me they don't like it."

"They don't like it?!" I was getting worked up and he tried to calm me down.

"You're acting like a loose cannon, they worry about giving someone like that a million pounds! You should be able to understand that!"

But I wasn't in a very understanding mood. Ever since Evie had quit and Felix had ended our friendship, I'd gone into a kind of emotional shutdown. I didn't talk to people unless I had to and kept interactions at a minimum. My patience was low and I seemed to snap and spit at people like a desert snake.

"Brits don't like this kind of attitude," he said to me, as politely as he could.

"What attitude is that?" I pretended not to know.

"Aggressive, direct, rude," Tim said.

I had another drink, felt the alcohol relaxing me. I'd taken my fasting to the next level too, sometimes fasting whole days. I thought it increased my mental energy, made my brain work twice as fast and well, but perhaps I was becoming a little wound too tight. I'd always been able to get along with people, especially in the tech sphere. It was the first time that a deal seemed to be in danger because of my personality.

On the third day, during a meeting about our future collaboration, the UK team proposed that a part of the project be developed in the UK. I saw this as a sign that they didn't trust us and was ready to call off the whole deal there and then. Tim managed to smooth things over and in the end, the agreement was signed.

On the flight back, I thought about how I'd almost wrecked the entire partnership because of what was going on in my life. It was becoming clear to me that denying my problems wasn't working. It was beginning to affect work and I couldn't allow that.

The desert retreat was supposed to fix everything.

But as I lay on my grass mat, listening to sound of drumming somewhere far away, I felt that being alone with my thoughts only made things worse. I kept thinking about Evie and how she wouldn't take my calls, wouldn't even respond to my text messages.

I'd gone to her place again to look for her, again encountering the room-mate who told me Evie had gone on some horse expedition.

"Horse riding?"

"That's right."

"But Evie doesn't like horses," I said, surprised.

"Lot of things about her you didn't know, I think," she said. Man, the girl hated me.

"Why won't she return my calls?" I asked her.

"I don't know. But my guess is, she don't wanna talk to you."

But why not, I wanted to ask her.

It made no sense to me that she didn't even want to talk to me? She'd said all along that I never talked to her, and here I was calling her every day and she couldn't pick up the phone?

I spoke to Summer one evening and she told me that Evie had called her.

That threw me. She'd speak to Summer but not to me?

"She says it's complicated."

I didn't think it was.

But it was clear to me that Evie didn't want to talk to me, so I decided to stop bothering her. I went to London and came back, trying to spend my time in the desert thinking not about work but about relaxing. Being mindful, whatever that was. My mind was full but not with the things I think it was supposed to be filled with. I kept thinking about Evie and thought a lot about LA when the two of us were together. It wasn't even supposed to be real, but it had felt that way at the time. We had talked about so many things, stuff I hadn't told anyone before. I didn't have to pretend at all. I did care about her. I do. Admitting it was a completely different thing altogether.

At the end of the silent retreat, there was a session with a kind of shaman-therapist person. The idea was to see if I had come up with insights and conclusions, if I'd had any strange dreams I wanted interpreting, that sort of thing.

All I wanted to know was, "Is there a vending machine around here? I need a Coke."

From experience, I knew that when my stomach was upset like this, I needed to drink Coke.

"My son," the shaman said, shaking his head. "What you need is lots and lots of something, but I'm not sure that that is Coke."

Whatever that meant.

I had a car pick me up and drive me home.

On the drive, I listened to messages and caught up on what was happening at work. Turned out they were coping well without me. Jill had gone off on leave, apparently needing a break too. I wasn't too surprised to hear that. Star left a message about the wedding, some details she needed. I let her know that Evie wasn't coming, that we'd broken up.

Second later there was a message from her: Sorry to hear that. She was nice.

When I didn't respond to that, she sent another message: Maybe too young?

But that wasn't it. I knew that wasn't the reason why things with Evie hadn't worked out. It was my fault, somehow. I didn't know how or why, but it was me. I didn't like the thought of it, though. It didn't sit well with me. Like a backpack where the weight was displaced, whenever I thought of Evie, I'd get this uncomfortable feeling. But what else could I do? I'd apologized, I'd tried calling. She wasn't at home.

I'd done all I could, right?

But, no.

I would come to work and look over at where she used to sit and I'd see my new PA, Melinda and feel disappointment in my gut. She wasn't Evie, in any way.

I'd go for dinner with Jacqueline and find my attention wandering. The last thing I felt like doing was to take her home, get her in bed.

One evening, in the car outside her place, Jacqueline had leaned over to kiss me. I had not seen it coming. It was a cheeky kiss, she pressed her body against mine and slipped her tongue into my mouth. Her hand wandered down to my groin, pressing on my cock and it responded the way she was expecting it too.

"Come up for coffee?" she asked, her voice inviting me to do much more than drink coffee. I went up to her place, a smart penthouse with a view over the bay. There was a thick fog over the water, blocking out the lights and the bridge. I knew it was out there, but I couldn't see anything.

"Hey there," she said and when I turned around, she was up and against me, kissing me and trying to get me in the mood. Jacqueline was beautiful, sophisticated and funny but it wasn't happening. I gently pushed her away.

"Not tonight," I said.

She bit her lip and turned away.

"It's not you..." I said and she nodded.

"I know," she said.

I wanted to want her but the truth was that the only woman I had any interest in, was Evie. Still. Even after I hadn't seen her for so long, I still wanted her.

This was new for me.

Jacqueline put on some clothes and brought me a drink.

"So, what's her name?" she asked me. There was a note of resignation in her voice.

I pretended not to know what she was taking about.

"It's obvious, Tate, there is someone else."

"No, there isn't."

"You've never pushed me away like that before," she said. Then, with a bit of sadness in her voice, she said, "A woman knows."

I couldn't tell her it was Evie, my former PA. How would that look?

"Whoever she is, she is a lucky woman," Jacqueline said with small smile on her full lips.

I thought Evie wouldn't agree.

Star wouldn't either.

It seemed the women in my life weren't all that lucky.

When I left Jacqueline's that night, I decided to give my ex a call.

Olga sounded asleep when she picked up the phone. I checked my watch and saw that it was after eleven.

"Did I wake you? I'm sorry."

"Tate, that you? Everything all right?"

I offered to call back another time but she said she was awake now.

"What's up? We haven't spoken in a while."

"I know, I've been busy, I guess. You okay?"

She told me about work and a new guy in her life. I was happy for her, genuinely.

Then I asked her, "I've been thinking about things, and I guess, I was wondering, if there was one thing I could have done to make things better between us, what would that be?"

Olga laughed softly. "You've fallen in love," she said.

"How do you know?" I didn't even try to deny it.

"It changes everything, doesn't it?" she said.

It was true, it felt like my whole life had been turned upside down.

"I think I've already screwed it up, to be honest," I said. "I don't even know what I did. I was just being myself. My nanny says I'm a cunt."

"I think that's a bit harsh," Olga said. "You are an entrepreneur and innovator, it's how you're wired."

"But does that mean I can't have relationships? A real connection?"

"No, that part is up to you," she said.

"But what do I do?" I asked.

Again, she laughed. "You do know what to do, you just don't know it. The language of love is not something you have to learn. We all know how to speak it."

"Christ," I said. "You sound like the podcast of one of those gurus from Hollywood that Star was always listening to."

Olga yawned. "It's late, I want to go back to bed. You've got this, Tate."

She put down the phone and I was left to mull over her words, feeling even more confused that when I spoke to her.

I couldn't believe how many people had written songs and poems and movies about being in love.

As far as I could tell, it totally sucked.

Chapter 23

E vie
The next couple of weeks pass in a bit of a blur.

I discover that I don't mind heights and I like hiking. I enjoy camping but I'm not fond of horses. I go for surfing lessons but after a couple of sessions out on the water, I decide that I will maybe go for another round in the summer. The weather is turning cold now and submerging myself in freezing temperatures isn't doing it for me.

I've started looking for a job again but the search is slow.

I don't want to work in a corporate environment, which is a bit of a tall order when Silicon Valley is fifteen minutes away. With a glowing reference from HumanITy's CEO, my resume is more interesting to recruiters now and I find invitations to interview for office jobs every week. But I'm not keen on those, or pretty much any of the jobs coming my way.

I prefer to hang out with the seniors at the center, taking them on their shopping trips and escorting them to their dental and medical appointments. I learn a lot about bunions and warts and cataracts and skin lesions.

One afternoon, I'm sitting at the hair salon waiting for Mrs. Hernandez to finish up her blowout when one of the hair stylists starts talking to me. I tell her I'm in between jobs and that I just resigned from being a PA to one of the big CEOs in Silicon Valley. She wants to know which one and when I tell her, the name clearly doesn't ring a bell. Then a guy in the chair across from me starts talking to me,

"You worked for Tate Sagarro?"

"Yup."

I can't see too much of this guy as he has his back to me and the stylist is snipping away at his hair.

"That must have been cool?" He has a warm, pleasant voice and for the first time in ages, I find myself not unwilling to chat about it. "It was, yeah. A bit crazy, but it was my first job so what did I know?"

When his hair is done, he gets up and comes to introduce himself, "I'm Carlos Aguero," he says. I estimate him to be in his forties, an attractive man in expensive jeans and a nice jacket. He sees me taking in his shoes. "I grew up in this neighborhood," he grins. "I still come here to get my hair cut. Keeps me humble," he says and winks at me, but in a friendly way.

"I may have a job opportunity for you if you're interested?"

He gives me his card and tells me to email him if I am. "It's not big bucks or anything, but we're looking for an office manager at our company. It's a gaming operation, not one of the big guys but we're growing. It's mostly administrative, keeping on top of the projects, that sort of thing."

It appeals to me right away.

His business card says he is the Chief Operating Officer and I decide I will email him and set up a coffee date.

On the way home, Mrs. Hernandez tells me all about Carlos Aguero. "I knew his mother, very nice lady. But his father.... Dios mío! He was a piece of work. Cheated on her, drank, was mixed up with all sorts of people. I think he died in jail."

She told me Carlos had a brother and a sister who lived with their mother a few blocks away.

"Few children are like that, you know," she said wistfully. I knew Mrs. Hernandez's daughter, Daisy, had moved to Los Angeles to make it in the film business. She'd found work as a stuntwoman, apparently, but was always on her way to an audition or heading out on location. She hardly ever visited.

That evening, I set up a coffee date with Carlos for the next day.

We met at his office, which wasn't exactly Silicon Valley and therefore exactly what I was looking for. The company consisted of about twenty people, mostly developers, a few marketing types and a couple of freelancers. I would be expected to co-ordinate with different employees, keep on top of all the projects, occasionally manage individual projects, sometimes set up meetings or organize lunches for the CEO. The current office manager had unexpectantly been admitted to hospital, they'd been waiting to see how serious it was, but Carlos had heard the day before that she needed a heart operation and would probably need several months off work. He was about to put up a job ad when he'd met me at the salon.

"If you don't mind my asking, why did you leave HumanITy?"

"It was personal," I admitted.

"I've heard he's demanding," Carlos said.

I didn't want to say anything else and Carlos respected that. I liked that about him. He told me he'd discuss it with the CEO and let me know. But I got a good feeling about it. The company specialized in Spanish games and mostly educational games for Spanish-speaking kids wanting to improve English language skills. It felt like something I wanted to be a part of.

Even Luisa was impressed to hear of the new job.

"I've heard of them," she said. "I played some of those games when I was little. So how is he, Carlos?"

"Nice," I said.

"Yeah, nice as in really nice or pretend nice and screw-you-over-later nice?" Luisa didn't have the full picture of what had happened with me and Tate. I'd never given her the details but I felt she had guessed almost all of it.

I shook my head. "No, he's nice. I like him. Not like that, mind you."

When he called to confirm the job appointment, I was happy.

I started a few days later and instantly felt comfortable at the company. Everyone was welcoming and friendly, I got the hang of their systems quickly and there weren't any weird dynamics or drastic deadlines. I was pleased to see that people mostly went home at the end of the day, they didn't look as frazzled or on-the-edge as they had at HumanITy.

Luisa came to visit me one day and I introduced her to Carlos, I could see there were sparks between them right away.

I remembered what that was like.

I had not forgotten about Tate Sagarro, even though I had tried to. Really hard.

I had gone out with Hector and even, briefly, dated a guy I'd met on a hang gliding adventure. His name was Craig, he worked in finance and was a very decent and good-looking individual with a lovely sense of humor. We went out a few times and I had a good time. He'd been keen to take things further but I didn't think it was fair. I still couldn't get Tate out of my head. Even though he had not sent me any messages in a long time and I was wondering if he was finally moving on. Every man I met was compared to Tate. Even if they were kinder, nicer, I would invariably find that I was unable to touch them. When Craig kissed me, I had to stop myself from recoiling from him in horror.

I still spoke to Summer. We had a regular date for Thursdays when Annika brought her for ice cream on their way home. At our last meeting, Summer told me about Star's wedding.

"It wasn't a real wedding," she said. "Star called it a 'commitment ceremony,'" she said making air quotes.

"Star was wearing white and she and Trevor held hands and read these really long poems to each other," she pulled a face. The reception was at a hotel in Malibu and the food was all vegan and totally inedible. "I asked Dad if we could go get MacDonalds and he said yes."

"To junk food?" I said, surprised.

"He says it's okay sometimes," Summer said matter-of-factly.

Annika looked at me, "Apparently some of his best friends eat MacDonalds and they're better than fine," she said with a wink.

I was about to ask who, then I realized, she meant me. He meant me.

The comment stuck with me, all the way home.

That evening, while Luisa was going on and on about Carlos and how wonderful he was and how did I manage to get any work done with such an attractive boss blah-blah-blah, all I could think about was Tate and how he was saying sweet things about me, even now, months after I'd left.

I checked my phone and found the messages he'd sent me in the weeks after I'd quit. There were voice messages I'd never listened to. The first couple were angry, typical Tate, demanding that I talk to him, insisting on this or that. Then, later, the messages became gentler, more sad. He wanted to talk, to apologize, to explain. After that, the messages became shorter, his voice was quiet. How was I doing, was I okay?

I'd never responded to any of them.

Now I sat with my phone, my heart beating fast.

I sent him a message: I hear some of your best friends eat McDonalds and they're fine?

Then I waited.

Chapter 24

T ate

After Summer has her dinner and goes up to her room, I hit the home gym for a serious session. I lift weights, do a bit of circuit and then hit the rowing machine for a set of punishing workouts. Sweat is pouring down my face and I feel my muscles burn as I push in and force myself to keep up the pace. I want to feel my limbs ache, to drive myself to the limit. By the time I get off the machine, my legs are jelly and I have to steady myself for a bit, drinking water to reenergize.

As I'm walking up to take a shower, I notice the message from my phone.

When I see who it's from, I stop.

It's from Evie.

The first message she has sent me since that night at the beach.

The words jump out at me from the screen and I read the sentence several times, letting them sink in so I can process them properly. After a minute, I realize that she's been talking to Summer. I know they've been meeting, of course. Annika told me after the first time, feeling guilty about doing something behind my back, worried she might get into trouble. Back then, I'd been mad at first, but then I realized it could be a good thing, not only for Summer to still have contact with Evie, but it was a way for me to not lose contact completely.

Annika knows, I think. She's been careful in how she does it but after meeting with Evie, she often makes casual remarks or says things to let me know how she's keeping. It will be behind Summer's back, so Summer does not know. Like if she's doing homework and Annika sees me coming in from outside, she'll motion to me to stop and loudly say something like, "Did you notice how sunburnt Evie was today?

From all that hiking she did?" Sometimes Summer would barely notice, and Annika would continue, "Don't you think it's funny she's doing all these outdoorsy things?"

This way, I got to know that Evie had not left San Francisco, that she was trying new things, which was good. I tried to listen out for mention of a boyfriend, something like that, but I knew better than to ask Summer or Annika outright.

But this text from Evie, it was big.

I knew it right away.

She was reaching out, sending me a message, letting me know that she was thinking about me too and maybe, was ready to start talking. It had been months since I'd seen her last. It wasn't easy to admit, but I had been struggling. I had feelings for Evie and I could do nothing about it. I wasn't used to taking the back seat, to stepping back, to giving someone space when I wanted to fill it.

But I had had to accept that this was the right thing to do here. I cared about Evie and this was what she wanted.

Until now.

I had a shower and thought about the response I wanted to send.

I thought more about that one sentence than I had thought about email messages to the heads of companies, the bosses at multimillion dollar corporations I wanted to do business with. Only a few words, but they were important, like messengers from the gods, they had to carry a very important message which I had to code in innocuous words, seemingly meaningless phrases. I had to make it sound like a joke, the way she had, use humor to mask my feelings. But it had to be clear that I appreciated her text and wanted to take it further, without coming on too strong.

This called for subtlety.

Not my strongest point.

So I soaped myself, I washed myself thoroughly, then I turned up the heat and at the last minute, blasted myself with cold water, waking myself up completely.

I needed every ounce of brain power I had here.

But it was hard, I couldn't find the right tone. The things I wanted to say, the emotion I wanted to convey. Time was passing by and I didn't want to wait too long. If I waited till morning, she could get the impression I had better things to do than text her back. Which was wrong, completely wrong. Nothing was more important to me right now.

In the end, my response seemed completely inadequate but it was the best I could come up with.

I sent back: Seems I was wrong about a lot of things. Total shock to the system.

I waited with bated breath.

It was after ten already, would she get it tonight? Would she respond? I waited for five minutes and the anxiety was getting to me. I jumped up and went downstairs to check on Summer, then walked through the house switching off lights and tidying things, looking at bills, opening actual physical mail, something I hadn't done, perhaps ever.

Evie didn't respond that evening, even though I was up for several hours, waiting for a response from her.

The next morning, her response came: You're not the only one. I got a few things wrong too.

I was quick with my answer: Not a lot, though.

She sent a smiley emoji face but no words.

Damn. I should have seen that coming. I didn't want to send something back too quickly but this is what I thought about all day. The fact that a channel of communication had finally been opened between us. It seemed like she was ready to talk to me again and I didn't want to blow it. I forced myself not to rush things, not my natural state at all.

But I had learned that there were things that felt right for me, that weren't. Steps of action that I would leap to, that were better not taken. Not if I wanted to keep people in my life, especially the ones that mattered.

By now, I had no doubt in my mind, if I could get Evie back in my life, I would do whatever I could and for the first time in months, it seemed possible.

I waited two days, then I sent the next message: I've learned a few things over the past few months. Wanna hear some of them?

Within minutes she answered: Don't drink and drive?

Keeping it light, I saw that.

I answered with the laughing tears emoji.

And waited. I was sure she would ask. But she kept me waiting a full day.

Then she sent: Ok. I'll bite...

I'd been thinking about this one for a while, so I was ready for her.

I said: I'm not as smart as I thought.

She texted: Oh?

Me: I lost you.

It was a bit of a gamble, I knew that. Coming on too strong, I could risk scaring her off again. But she had to know that I still cared about her, perhaps more than ever. I couldn't pretend to have a light, meaningless interaction with her like I sat next to her in chemistry class in school. I wanted her to know that I still wanted her. That I was sorry and that I would do anything to get her back.

She responded the same night: I'm not lost.

To which I responded: Best news I've had all day.

Our texts increased in frequency and we started texting every day. Sometimes in the morning, sometimes at night. I never called her, even though I wanted to. She didn't suggest it either. This was comfortable for both of us, for now. I learned that she had a new job, I told her my new PA had ADHD and kept forgetting to give me my messages but I was practicing my new mantra for kindness. She found this hysterical and I could pretend that she hurt my feelings. I told her I'd appointed a Chief Operating Office to take over the day-to-day running of things so I could concentrate on innovation. She said her new boss and room-mate were hooking up. This was dangerous territory.

Me: How do you feel about that?

Her: What do you think?

Me: They're not in the same office, though?

Her: No. But he's a nice guy

Me: Where did he train? Or was he born that way?

Her: (Laughing emoji)

About three weeks after we started texting again, I asked if she wanted to go for lunch. I made a joke, promising not to talk about work or any serious topics.

Her: What else is there to talk about?

Me: Are you kidding? Summer? Star's vows? New hiking trails?

Her: Ok

I just wanted to see her again. I wanted to get a sense of whether there was something between us that could be salvaged, fixed, patched up again. If I had a shot at getting her back into my life somehow. The fact that she'd contacted me was a good sign, I knew that.

I proposed a sushi restaurant near her work.

I made sure to be there when she got there, sitting in a window seat so I could watch her arrive and have a few moments at least to prepare. But she didn't come. Five minutes passed, then another five. Bitterness coursed through me, disappointment so big I could barely swallow or breathe. It was followed by anger, which I knew by now, to be the wrong response. I waited half an hour before I was willing to admit that she wasn't coming.

I couldn't believe it. I had been so sure that everything would work out this time, that this was going to be the break we needed. I was hungry but I couldn't eat. I didn't want to drink. I wasn't used to rejection, to losing. It seemed like when it came to Evie, I couldn't win, no matter what I did.

Was this something I had to accept?

My entire being said no, I wasn't made that way.

I fought for what I wanted.

But as I stared out at the empty street outside the restaurant, I thought maybe the time had come to stop fighting a losing battle.

Chapter 25

E vie
I was about to leave for lunch when Carlos came out towards me.

"Do you have a minute?" he asked me. His face was tense, which was unusual. Carlos was laid-back, relaxed, easy-going. Since I'd started working there, I'd never seem him lose his temper with anyone.

"Of course."

I looked at my watch and saw I had a few minutes. Carlos probably wanted an update on one of the many projects we had going. This wouldn't take long. I'd wanted to go into the ladies to check on my hair before I left. This lunch with Tate was big. There was no denying it. The first time we saw each other in months and after weeks of texting. The anticipation had been building, I'd been waiting for him to suggest it and when he finally did, I was so relieved, I had yelled out loud for joy.

But I couldn't let Carlos down.

He'd given me this job, treated me better than any boss had until now. True, I didn't have much to compare him to, just a crazy Silicon Valley exec and the grumpy old geezer up in Lake Tahoe where I'd worked in the restaurant kitchen.

Still. I closed the door behind me so that Carlos and I were alone in his office.

"What's up?"

"This may be awkward for you," Carlos began and I immediately thought, oh no. This wasn't about one of the projects. For a terrible moment, I thought he was going to confess his undying love for me, which would have been a disaster.

But then he said. "It's Luisa." He had an anguished look on his face and I felt truly sorry for him.

"Ah," I said, nodding. "Of course."

"We've started seeing each other, as you know," he said and I kept nodding, because of course, I knew. She'd been seeing him mostly over weekends, Carlos would take her out to restaurants, sometimes she stayed the night at his place, a luxury apartment near the Bridge. But I knew Luisa was seeing other guys too, going out with her usual crowd of friends who liked to drink and dance. A younger crowd, to be honest. After the first few dates, I could tell that even though she really liked Carlos, it was probably not going to work out. But looking at Carlos's anguished face, I could see that he wanted more.

"Just a moment," I said, taking out my phone to quickly text Tate that I was going to be late.

Then I put the mobile away.

"I thought things were going well," he said in a strained voice. "I even took her to meet my mother, but lately, I don't know, I've been getting a bad feeling. She's not returning my calls, she says she's too busy with her studies to go out?"

"It's her last year, you know, there are many assignments, tests and so on," I said, even though I knew that wasn't it.

Carlos was pacing up and down the office. "I thought we had something, you know?"

There were tears in his eyes. It was painful to see.

"She's too young for you, Carlos," I suddenly said. "Let her go."

"What?" He stopped pacing, stared at me.

I got up and walked up to him. Sometimes, it was better to rip the plaster right off. Prolonging the agony was going to make it all worse in the long run.

"Luisa is 21, she wants to stay up all night to party, she doesn't want to sit at home and watch The Voice."

I saw him blink, processing the fact that she'd told me this was the show he liked to watch.

"But... but... she liked it, she told me she loved it!!" he almost wailed in despair.

"She hates it," I said. "Look, Carlos, you're an amazing guy. The best boss I've ever worked for. If I wasn't hung up on someone else, who knows, I might have fallen for you. Please don't waste time on someone who is not right for you."

He had turned away from me, his shoulders twitching and I had the horrible feeling he was crying. I didn't want to see a grown man cry. Especially not my boss, and someone I respected hugely.

"You might have fallen for me?" he turned to face me. Of course that would have been the one part of that speech that he'd heard! "Yes, you old fool, of course I would. You're handsome and successful and such a nice guy! You don't know how rare that is! Cut your losses, move on. Luisa's not worth it."

"Luisa is your friend?" He sounded confused.

"I know and I love her, dearly. But for you, it's not right. Luisa likes to play around, she likes to have fun, be a little wild. Maybe your relationship has run its course?"

I could see Carlos was processing this, and working his way into accepting it.

He stood a little straighter, took a deep breath.

"God, you must think I'm such a loser," he said, unable to meet my eye.

"Of course not!" I walked over to him and touched his arm. "I've learnt something over this past year. Brutal honesty is better than telling yourself all kinds of stories that make you feel better but aren't true. I think you are a catch, a total winner. But you and Luisa aren't right for each other. The moment you realize that and move on, you can find the woman you should be with."

He nodded slowly. "Perhaps you're right," he said, in a sad voice.

"I know I'm right." I gave his arm a squeeze. "And now I'm late for lunch, see you later."

I rushed out of the office, practically running down the stairs.

I checked my watch and saw that I had spent over half an hour in there. I couldn't believe it! There was not time to check my outfit or to see if my hair was fine. I struggled to get an Uber driver and by the time I arrived at the restaurant, the lunch hour was almost up. My heart sank when I saw the time.

I'd really looked forward to seeing him again.

But there was no way he'd be waiting for me this long. Not Tate Sagarro. He had meetings to go to, emails to send, projects to greenlight. People to fire. He didn't hang around for girls who were late to lunch dates.

I walked into the restaurant, sighing deeply as I pushed open the door.

I was about to ask the staff if he'd been there and how long he'd waited, then I spotted a familiar figure at a booth in the corner. It was his hair I recognized first, the shaggy blonde hair. Then the broad shoulders and the unmistakable aura that pulsed around Tate Sagarro. He was leaning back against the upholstery, it seemed his eyes were closed.

Was he sleeping? That didn't seem right?

"Tate?" I leaned closer, touched his shoulder.

I Iis eyes flew up and he jumped upright

"You came!" A huge grin spread over his face. "You came!"

I pulled a face, "Just an hour late, but yeah..." I sat down opposite him, at the table.

"You got my message?"

"What message?"

I looked at my phone and saw that I had sent it to someone else by mistake.

"It doesn't matter," Tate said, "You're here now."

A waiter came to take our order and turned around when he saw Tate grabbing my hands and holding them tightly.

"I'm sorry about everything. Being late for lunch today, but also before that, not getting back to you for weeks, not letting you know where I kept the slides for the UK presentation, not sending you some reports from my laptop," the words all came tumbling out in one big torrent.

Tate laughed, relieved. "I don't care about any of that."

"You don't?"

He shook his head. "I think I love you, Evie, I can't think about anything else. Please come back to me."

"As your PA?" I was confused.

He smiled, "No, I want us to be together. Boyfriend, girlfriend, partner, whatever you want to call it."

I heard the words but I couldn't quite believe them. It was what I wanted to hear, wasn't it? Then why did it feel so unreal?

"I know a lot has happened, and we need to work through it." He took a deep breath. "That's why I've been thinking: No sex. Let's just get to know each other first. We'll wait with the rest. What do you say? I see you like hiking now? Let's go for a hike this weekend? What do you say?"

No sex?

I looked at Tate, incredulously, "No sex?"

He grinned. "I know, sounds insane, right, what else is there?"

He was being ironic, though, I could tell.

"Absolutely, what on earth would we do when we were together?"

"We could eat," he suggested.

"But only when you're not fasting, right, which is what, between six and two in the afternoon?"

I looked at my watch. "I think we've just missed that window by a minute! Did you eat already?"

Tate winked at me. "I'm going to take a break from the exercise regime and the fasting. Going on a little holiday from all that. What do you say, shall we have lunch? Maybe a burger, with fries? Preferably deep fried in a gallon of dirty palm oil?"

I laughed.

Tate called the waiter over and we ordered hamburgers.

We stayed for two hours. Just talking about everything, Star's wedding-that-wasn't-a-wedding, Summer's new friend at school, a girl called Maddie who liked horses and everything that was the color green; how he was taking it easier at work. He asked me about my new job and Carlos, and about all the adventures I'd done over the past few weeks.

"You were right," I said. "I needed to loosen up a bit, take some chances."

"I'm serious about the hike," he said. "Have you seen the redwoods yet? I know a good place to go."

"Sounds great," I said.

I couldn't believe we were sitting here, in a fairly average restaurant, on plastic leather seats, having eaten normal hamburgers, not on artisanal bread with some kind of imported duck butter or anything over the top like that. Just ordinary burgers.

"I have to go to work now," I said, a little regretfully.

"Your new boss sounds tough," Tate said, getting up.

"It's nothing like my old boss," I said, stealing a glance at Tate.

"What was he like?" Tate asked in a light voice.

"Wonderful," my voice caught as I choked on the emotion I was feeling.

Tate swooped down and kissed me then, pulling me close in front of everyone at the restaurant. But I didn't notice any of that. I was consumed by joy, feeling his arms around me, his warm, spicy smell surrounded me and I knew, without a fact, that I had come home. I was finally where I needed to be.

Chapter 26

Tate

It was winter now but I didn't feel the cold.

I had Evie to keep me warm. We took it slow, like, tectonic plate movement slow. For a few weeks, we held hands and kissed, nothing past first base. I felt like I was in school again, a teenager with raging hormones, dreaming of getting into some hot girl's pants. The funny thing was, it wasn't Evie who was stopping things from moving further. It was me. I was the one pulling back, saying hold on, let's take a minute.

She never disagreed with me although I often wished she would.

I wanted to show her that I could have a relationship without sex, that it wasn't all about being physical for me. But I ached for her, to feel her body against mine again. I knew what it was like, after all, to be with her, and nothing else came close. Well, it did come close and I knew we were leading up to it. I could see it in her eyes, her lingering touches, the way she touched my thigh sometimes. She'd look at me, teasingly, waiting for me to make the next move and I didn't. We went for walks on beaches, saw movies, went to restaurants, took Summer to skate parks and had ice cream at the beach. It was like ticking every box on a dating site checklist.

One night, dropping her off at her place after we'd gone to dinner, she asked if I wanted to come up. The way she'd said it, her voice low and suggestive, made it obvious what she was talking about. "My room-mate is out, so we'll have the place to ourselves?"

I didn't need to be asked twice.

We went up the stairs, giggling like teenagers, me trying to pull her in for kisses along the way and her trying to wriggle free and get away from me, but not really. At the door, struggling with her keys, I asked her, "Are you sure?"

"About what?" she winked at me. "The future, us, the meaning of life? No! But let's not overthink this, yeah? It's been long enough."

I couldn't have agreed with her more.

We went straight to bed, getting rid of our clothes as quickly as we could, then jumping under the covers as it was freezing. Evie's bed was a basic double bed, the sheets were nothing like my imported cotton and silk blends, but none of that mattered. When I took her into my arms, felt her skin against mine, there was nothing between us anymore. I kissed her for a long time, exploring her all over again, tasting her neck and licking her ear lobe, nibbling at the soft, tender skin. I let my hands wander all over her body, feeling her slightly tighter muscles, the more toned arms. She groaned as my hands slid between her legs and I touched her there, sliding my fingers into her pussy, caressing her, stroking slowly but insistently, feeling for her clitoris and gently rubbing it. I went down on her, eager to taste her, to lick and kiss her. She opened her legs wide and I buried my face in her, enveloped by the most intoxicated smell of her. She moaned and groaned as I probed with my tongue, licking and sucking, and she moved her hips against me, demanding more. When she came, it was with a scream of delight that pierced the quiet air in the apartment.

"Oh my God," she said, over and over again, as I slipped my cock inside of her, so incredibly turned on that I climaxed right away.

"That was incredible," she said in a low voice.

"Worth waiting for?" I asked.

"Without a doubt."

I wanted to spend the night but I didn't want Summer waking up and I wasn't there. She'd been delighted to hear that Evie and I had made up and that she was back in my life. But when I said we were dating, I could see that was confusing. She didn't quite know what to make of that, so for her sake, Evie wasn't spending nights there and we tried not to be too overt with displays of affection.

We were taking small steps, taking nothing for granted.

I took Evie and Summer for a visit at my brother Brett's wine farm in Napa Valley. We were not close but I thought it might be nice to get away and for Summer to see her cousins. Summer hadn't been there in years. The farm was beautiful, a French-style Tuscan affair built of stone with wide views of the hills. Brett's wife, Nadine, had inherited money from her father and when Brett was tired of trying his hand at politics in DC, they'd come down to Napa to grow grapes. Their pinot noir was not bad at all. Brett was five years older than me, sometimes it felt more like twenty. It had always been hard for us to get along, we were just too different.

But this was a good weekend.

As soon as we'd arrived, the cousins came to show Summer the stables and the new foal that had been born the week before. Nadine gave Evie a big hug and insisted on showing her the house. Brett and I went outside, he told me about work, asked how I was doing. Dinner was a huge and noisy affair, the boys arguing and Summer laughing and us drinking too much wine.

Afterwards, while the women cleared the table, I helped Brett get wood for the fireplace outside.

"Evie is lovely," he said, glancing at me. "But she's..."

"Young?" I suggested. That always seemed to come up when people talked about us.

"No," he shook his head with a smile. "I was going to say normal."

I pretended to be hurt.

"I'm not normal?"

Brett gave me a look. "Bro, you're many things, but normal is not one of them. Remember that teacher at school who said you were a free radical?"

I remembered that. I had thought it was a compliment at the time, until I later learnt more about chemistry and realized it had not been intended to flatter me. He meant that I was unstable, that I could damage people, and myself. At the time, I had been a rebellious teenager and perhaps, it had been a fair comment. The one thing I liked about free radicals, was that they were capable of independent existence. For a long time, there was nothing else I'd wanted more than to be left to do my own thing, even in a relationship. But Evie had changed that. I no longer wanted to be alone anymore.

"I mean Star wasn't normal, even before you got married. And I'm thinking of that girlfriend you had in high school, Cassie? Didn't she go on to do some weird stuff?"

I was trying to keep my cool, I didn't want to get into an argument.

"Cassie is an installation artist in New York, she does well. I've seen her work. I don't always understand it, but she's done well for herself," I said.

Brett wanted to say something else and I interjected, "Look, I know what you mean, Brett, but I've changed, okay? I'm not the man I used to be."

He bit his lip and nodded. "You realize she's going to want to get married, have kids, the whole shebang?"

I nodded but I did feel something shift.

I hadn't thought about that specifically, no. Now that he'd mentioned it, I wondered about it. I hadn't enjoyed the marriage experience that much. Or at all, to be honest. Not that I'd ever wanted to get married in the first place. But there had been a time in the beginning, in that first year when Star and I had gotten to know each other, when I thought she was the only woman for me. I wouldn't have called it love. But in a way, we fitted together, it worked, for a while. When she proposed one night, both of us stoned, having waited for the dawn to break over the mountains in some off-the-beaten-track location, it had seemed like a great idea. A crazy idea, sure, but I was all about the crazy ideas. Especially back then, I didn't worry too much about things failing, not working out.

"We tell the rest of the world to go fuck themselves, it's just you and me from now on."

It wasn't the most romantic of proposals, but I had liked it. I had liked our wedding too, and when we moved in together, that had been groovy. Then, she got pregnant and had the baby and suddenly, nothing was good anymore. We weren't sleeping, the baby was always crying and she hated the way she looked and the fact that I was always leaving to go to work. I couldn't wait to get away from all that, to be honest. Bury myself in code, forget about the dirty kitchen and the screaming wife.

The thought of having to go through all that again, that was a sobering thought.

When we left the next morning after breakfast, there were warm hugs all round.

"Don't wait so long before you come again," Brett said.

As we drove off, Summer told us how they'd played games all night long. She was excited, said she and one of her cousins had exchanged email addresses and would be playing again online.

"What's up?" Evie asked me as we got home.

"Nothing," I said.

"You haven't said a word the whole way back."

I shrugged.

"Would you prefer it if I went home?"

"What? No." I took a breath and blurted out, "It's something my brother said, about you'd be wanting to get married and have kids."

Evie smiled. "And get a wine farm in Napa and a wife who needs to go on holiday twice a year to escape from it all?"

I chuckled, remembering the story Brett had told us at dinner last night. It had been a joke, he'd been teasing Nadine but there was an undercurrent there that I had picked up on, Evie too. Even in paradise, life was not simple, it seemed.

She came up to me, put her arms around my waist, kissed my cheek.

"I haven't thought about any of that, to be honest. It's not important to me."

"But it might be, one day?" I asked.

"And that would be, terrible?"

"I don't know," I admitted. "The first time round was pretty bad, to be honest."

"How bad," Evie asked. "Scale of one to ten?"

"About a hundred and four?"

She smiled sadly.

"Then we don't go there."

"Really?" I wondered if she could give up on all of it, just like that. She was young, as everyone kept pointing out.

"It's early days for us," Evie said with a soft smile.

"I know," I said, leaning down to kiss her. "I'm just so happy right now with how everything is going, I don't want anything to wreck it."

"I'm happy too," she said, kissing me back. "I love you."

Just like that, the dark mood brought on by Brett's ominous words disappeared. Like clouds drifting out of my sky.

Chapter 27

E vie
I spend Christmas at home. My brother comes down from Washington and brings his new girlfriend India along. There is not enough room in the cabin for all of us and we end up having to share couches and mattresses on the floor of my parents' place. India is uptight and clearly nervous about meeting all of us and my father's forced friendliness and my younger brother's joking demeanor don't make it any easier. On Christmas Eve, my mother tries to get India to open up a bit while we're preparing dinner but it falls flat.

"Did you grow up in Washington?" she asks India.

"Not really," she says, without elaborating.

"So, outside of Washington then?" My mother persists.

India is peeling potatoes and she seems lost in her thoughts. After a moment, she picks up that both my mother and I are staring at her, waiting for an answer. "Uhm, yes, a little town a few hours away."

She offers no more information. I can see my mother struggling with this conversation.

"We used to live in Washington before we came out here," I offer. "But Andy's probably told you all about that?"

She smiles at me and says, "Yes."

My mom is making big eyes at me and so I decide to make the whole situation less uncomfortable by talking about my new job and how it is going in the city.

"And how's the boyfriend?" my mother asks.

I told her about Tate and I getting together without too much of the details. She knows that he used to be the boss at my old company and that we had gotten to know each other there. I never provided specifics on how we got to know each other or how well, exactly. But she'd guessed that he was the "senior executive" I'd been seeing for a while.

"Things are good, we're happy," I say and it's true.

"How long have you been together?" India asks me, for the first time interested in something about me.

"It was a bit on and off but properly together? About two months."

"We still haven't met him, though," my mother says pointedly. "Kind of makes me wonder if you are ashamed of us or ashamed of him?" I think she meant it as a joke, but India reacts immediately, looking at me and my mother.

"I'm obviously ashamed of you!" I say quickly, "I mean, he is perfect so it can't be him."

India's eyes widen in horror and I realize I'm making it worse. She does not know we're joking.

Later, after we've finished eating and cleaning up, India and I are making up beds on the sofa in the living room, settling down for the night. Then India suddenly says, "I grew up in foster care. I never knew my parents."

"I'm sorry to hear that," I say, not sure how to respond.

"My foster parents were kind people, but much older. I was the only child. It was very quiet in the house."

Now I know where she's going with this. "I'm afraid our house is a bit loud," I say apologetically. "That's kind of how it is with brothers. They're always teasing and joking and trying to prank you."

I tell her how when I was a teenager, Steve had pretended to be a boy from school, sending me messages on my phone, telling me he liked me and would I come meet him at night in the woods. I did, of course, and no one showed. Then Steve came to get me and laugh at me.

"That's horrible," India says.

"Yeah," I say. "But I knew it was him all along, so it wasn't too bad. And I got my revenge."

"What did you do?"

"I signed him up for a musical at the school and he got one of the leads. He couldn't pull out because he liked this one girl and he'd be doing the show with her. But he was furious with me because all his jock buddies made fun of him for the rest of the year. Called him Justin, after Justin Bieber, you know?"

She smiled.

I could see that she was trying to understand how our family worked. It was one of the reasons why I was slow to introduce Tate to my family. I knew they would be in awe of him, once they knew who he was and I feared he wouldn't handle it too well either, he wasn't really good in stressful situations with people who were important. It had taken us almost a year to get together, so I knew. I had no intention of introducing my folks to Tate before I was sure that all of us were ready for it.

"You guys look happy, though," I said. "Andy is more relaxed than I've ever seen him. But that may just be the beard."

My eldest brother had always been a bit more straight-laced, certainly more responsible than Steve. He wasn't one for drinking and going out as much and was closer to my mother. She'd taken it hard when he'd chosen not to make the move to Lake Tahoe with us. Once he finished school and went to college, we saw even less of him, mostly over the holidays.

"The beard was his idea," India said with a little laugh. "I don't like it, makes him look old."

I tell her Steve used to call him "old man", said he was old before his time. He never liked that much.

India smiled, "He told me that." She paused. "He said he struggled to find his place in the family, always felt like the odd man out." She said they had met each other at the gym, after both wanted the same exercise bike. He told her to take it and she insisted that he take it. Afterwards, they had a smoothie in the health bar and that was when everything started. Her voice softened when she talked about Andy and with a pang, I realized that she really loved him. When my mother, after Christmas, asked me what I thought about her, I said I thought India was the best thing that had happened to my brother.

Then Tate took me on a holiday after Christmas.

He'd gone snowboarding with friends and then we flew out to Colorado to a luxury resort where we had our own cabin tucked into the mountains. It was gorgeous, intimate and very romantic. I could ski but had never really tried snowboarding. Tate wanted to show me, insisted that it was the best adrenaline rush and how I would love it once I'd tried it. I wasn't so sure, but I kept this information to myself.

He insisted on teaching me himself, which I thought was because he just wanted to stand close to me, pretending to help me get the moves right while really trying to grope me. It was fun though, standing on the beginner slopes, surrounded by kids whizzing past me like Olympic athletes while I could barely stand up without falling down.

"It's hopeless!" I said after falling down one too many times, face down in the snow. I took off my goggles and hat and tried wiping my face. But my gloves were wet, everything was full of snow and I was just making it worse.

"Can we please go back and have some hot chocolate?"

"One more time," Tate said. "Come on, you're so close to getting the basic moves."

I agreed to try one more time, standing up carefully and bouncing on the board to a level spot where I could try get a bit of movement. My legs hurt from all the falling down, my elbow throbbed from where I had stubbed it a moment ago and I took a deep breath to steady me. The incline was very mild and I wouldn't go too fast. I thought about Tate's instructions and pushed my feet down to get the board moving. I felt it starting to slide and turned my hips slightly when all of a sudden, everything went haywire and I was flying through the air like a ragdoll.

"Oh, my God, are you all right?" Someone was calling out to me. I opened my eyes and tried to figure out where I was. I was on my back, staring at the sky. I turned my head and saw someone crawl to me on hands and knees, awkwardly, because of a snowboard strapped to one leg.

"Are you okay?" It was Tate, on my other side, helping me sit up.

"I'm fine," I was laughing now, finally getting my wind back. "All good."

"I thought I'd killed you!" The woman pulled off her hat and glasses and grabbed my hands. She was middle-aged, probably as old as my mother, and kept saying over and over again how sorry she was. Her husband came running down. "Are you all right?" He asked me. Only then did he look at his wife. "Lordy lord, Steph, didn't I say go left, go left! You kept going right!"

"I know!" she wailed. "I don't know why!"

"It's coz you're always mixing up your left and right!"

"I know, I know!" she was crying uncontrollably and the husband came to hug her. "It's okay, hon. You're okay, she's okay, we're all okay, right?"

"I'm okay," I confirmed with a smile.

"You tried, hon, that's the best any of us can do right?"

"So can I stop trying now?" she asked him.

"Well," he said. "If you're fine with it. This was your idea remember? I said let's go fishing in Florida but no, you were all about the skiing. Remember?"

"I remember," she said miserably. "I don't know what I was thinking. Trying to do this at my age! I almost killed someone!"

I was laughing now, the whole situation struck me as very funny.

"You're really okay?" she looked at me with deep concern as if she thought I was lying to her and secretly bleeding to death.

I started laughing and then she and her husband started laughing too.

"It's really fine, you guys, honest."

We went back to our chalet for a warm bath, red wine and some careful, slow sex that didn't involve my knees or elbows or any action around my butt area.

That evening, after a candlelit dinner set up in our own private dining area, we moved to the cozy fireplace where pillows and throws made a very comfy little sitting area. Tate and I cuddled together on the sofa.

"Are you okay, because I'm okay," Tate said, mimicking the couple from the ski slope.

We laughed again.

"Do you think we're going to be like that when we're fifty?" I asked him. "Still going to do fun things, trying out new stuff?"

"I hope so," Tate said, suddenly serious.

"I have the best time with you."

"Me too," I said, leaning forward to kiss him.

"Will you marry me?" he suddenly asked.

"What?" I wasn't expecting this.

"I want you by my side when I'm fifty, I want to be that couple, laughing and rolling around in the snow, loving each other no matter what."

"Me too," I said. "Of course I'll marry you."

Chapter 28

Tate

The wedding proposal didn't come quite out of the blue.

Over Christmas, when most people spend time with their families, I went off snowboarding with two college buddies. Summer went to LA to visit Star and I flew to Canada to a remote location where Matt, Joe and I had regularly gathered since we'd been in college. We aimed for once a year, but sometimes life got in the way. So, it wasn't unusual that we'd skipped the year before and I was looking forward to catching up with them and hitting some serious snow.

But things didn't go quite as planned.

The past two years seemed to have taken their toll on the guys. A property developer, Matt had picked up at least thirty pounds as well as a lot of debt, due to some problems with a bad investment. Joe, on the other hand, was gaunt and almost skeletal. He worked in finance, loved spending money and the high life. He had a hedonistic, no-strings-attached philosophy about everything in life. He lived in the moment, he liked to say, nobody to depend on or who depended on you. I'd always related to this world view but I found I didn't anymore. Falling in love had changed everything about me.

I wasn't keen to tell the guys this but one evening, after a particularly grueling day out on the mountain, we started drinking whiskey and opened up a bit more than usual. Matt had bailed on us, not being in the shape he used to be, he'd struggled to keep up with Joe and I. But I also had the feeling Joe was pushing himself too much, trying to pull moves and do tricks like he was trying to prove something.

After a few drinks, Matt told us he'd stopped drinking and smoking. "Lucy was going on about how unhealthy it was. The next minute, I had this," he patted his stomach and pulled a face, "Much worse, if you ask me."

"What's that, like five burgers a day?" Joe asked and Matt shook his head, "Fuck you, man. We can't all live off cocaine and energy drinks."

Joe glowered at him. "At least I don't have to listen to a wife telling me to sit and roll over and be a good boy any time I want to get laid."

Matt groaned. "Oh man, you still want to go at it every day? What're you, a teenager?"

Joe grabbed his groin, "Listen, this puppy has to play every day, know what I mean?"

They were talking like kids, high on hormones and bad self-esteem.

"What about you, Sagarro?" Joe asked.

I didn't want to talk about Evie like that and got up to get more booze.

"I'm actually thinking of getting married again," I said and waited for the avalanche of ridicule to begin. There was a moment of silence and then it began.

"No way! Why would you do that to yourself again?" Joe asked.

"God, really?" Matt said. He'd married his college sweetheart Lucy and had always seemed happy to me. But the kids and the mortgages, the holidays and the ballet lessons, music classes and private school tuition was finally getting to him. "I don't even have money to buy beer," he complained.

"I love her," I said and shrugged, almost embarrassed to admit it.

Then I saw their faces. Both of them, had envy written all over their faces. They wanted what I had. Not the money or the success. But the love, they didn't have that, or not anymore.

The next morning, when Joe and I got up early to try a new rockface, we left Matt to lie in. We set out on a back road, carrying our boards, walking up through the snow. We reached the top of the mountain and looked out over the snow-covered trees and valley. It was beautiful. An isolated, untouched wilderness and we were going to plough through it with our boards. I couldn't wait to get to it but then Joe said, quietly, "I get it you know. You should go for it."

I didn't know what he was talking about, but then he said.

"The girl. If it's love, go for it."

I nodded.

Without looking at me, he told me how he had been in an accident over a year ago. A car knocked him over and he had a bad fall, induced by doctors into a coma. But he had listed some girlfriend from years ago as his emergency contact and she'd changed her number, so they couldn't get hold of anyone. "My bosses thought I'd gone off on a bender," he said. "They basically fired me, I lost a whole lot of deals, cost the company millions. By the time I woke up, I had basically lost my life. And I was close to no-one. Couldn't exactly list my dealer as my nearest and dearest."

It was a lot to take in.

"What I'm saying is, real love is rare. If that is what you have, grab it with both hands and don't let anyone change your mind."

I came back from that trip, and on a whim, decided to surprise Evie at her parents' house. She'd decided to stay on after Christmas and Summer was still with Star. I knew there were a lot of people at the home and booked into a place at Lake Tahoe. But I figured it was a good time to meet her family. I knew I wanted to commit to Evie, I wanted her in my life for good and that meant knowing her family and somehow, having them in my life too.

I got there the day after Christmas, during the afternoon.

I knocked on the door and heard the sound of the TV and a game being watched and men commenting loudly on what was happening on the screen.

Evie's mom opened the door. I knew it was her because I could see Evie's features in her, the same petite face and blonde hair, the porcelain blue eyes.

"Hello?" she said, open and friendly, just like Evie was.

"I'm Tate Sagarro," I said, sticking out my hand. "I think it's time we met."

She smiled and yelled over her shoulder. "Evie, your fella's here!"

From deep within the cabin, I heard Evie say, "What? No he's not."

I enjoyed the look on her face when she saw me on the doorstep.

"What are you doing here?"

"I heard your mother's lasagna was to die for," I said. Suddenly one of the brothers appeared next to the mother, dwarfing her with his size. "You mean, you could die from her lasagna. Did you know she actually killed someone once with that food?"

"Steve!" the mother admonished him. "How was I to know that girl was allergic to nuts!"

"Who puts nuts in lasagna?!" Steve went on. "I mean, no recipe calls for it?"

"Who follows recipes, anyway," I said, and seeing the gratitude in Evie's mothers eyes made up for possibly alienating Steve. "Following recipes is for people with no imagination."

Before the situation could escalate, Evie was right there, giving me a hug.

"What are you doing here?"

"I missed you," I said. It was true. The thought of being alone in my big house without anyone there was not inviting. I would rather be here, with Evie, than by myself. That was a first.

I went in, met Evie's father and other brother and got pulled into a heated debate about the NFL and who was going to win the championship. The next morning, her father took me out to show me his boat. "So, you and Evie..." he said, looking at me.

"Yes, Sir," I said.

"You're a..." again he didn't finish his sentence, but looked at me seriously. He was a big man, just like his son, Steve, but his eyes were kind. Despite the gruff appearance and raspy voice, I had the feeling he was a softie.

"Yes," I said, resolutely. "I am."

Even though he didn't come outright and ask me what my intentions were, I knew that was what he was doing. And I was telling him that I would do right by her, in my own way.

"She's my little girl," he said, and suddenly, he was tearing up, having to turn away so I didn't see the tears in his eyes.

"Yes, Sir," I said.

"You know, I would..." I had to imagine what he meant to say, I thought he probably meant he'd knock me down if I hurt her.

"Yes, Sir," I said.

His other son Andy arrived. He had a slimmer build than his father and brother, but the same eyes as Evie and her mother. Blue and empathetic, sensitive. He came over to talk to me as we walked back from the house.

"He almost shot a boy who made her cry once," Andy said, looking over his shoulder. "Turned out the boy didn't even know what was going on. One of Stevie's pranks, pretending to be the boy and sending dirty messages to Evie. Dad almost got into trouble for that."

"Wow," I said, trying to imagine Evie's father with a shotgun on my doorstep.

"What I'm trying to say is, he's an ask-questions-later sort of guy."

"I get it," I said. "I've made mistakes but I'm making less of them now."

"Sounds good," Andy said.

When we got to the house, Evie was watching me carefully.

"What did you talk about with my brothers?" she asked.

"Nothing," I said.

But it was her mother who proved to be the biggest obstacle after all. When Evie went to go pack, she cornered me in the kitchen.

"You didn't treat her right," she said in an even tone, which threw me.

"Pardon?"

"She worked for you and you were mean to her."

Had Evie told her that? I wondered.

"Evie didn't tell me, in case you're wondering. I figured it out for myself. I know what it looks like when you get your heart broken."

I could've pretended it wasn't me, or come up with a story. But I didn't.

"Yeah... that was... I'm not proud of that."

She gave me a hard look.

"It took me a while to realize that I was losing the best thing that ever happened to me."

Evie came into the kitchen. "What's happening here? Mom?"

Her mother smiled and punched me on the shoulder, a little hard, come to think of it.

"Oh, nothin'. Just givin' him some third degree."

Evie looked uneasy but I smiled at her. These people cared about her, they really loved her and I could appreciate that.

We went up to a resort for a little holiday after that, just the two of us before Summer came back. I wanted to teach Evie to snowboard, maybe practice some new moves. I'd found us a luxury resort where we could have our own cabin and meals and didn't have to rub shoulders with families or young guys come to get drunk and spoil everyone else's time.

Maybe it was everything leading up to that point, the weird weekend with Joe and Matt and then getting grilled by Evie's parents, all of it made me realize that I really wanted to be with her. In every way. Even the boring, uncomfortable ways that I never would have considered before. I wanted to be her plus one, her emergency contact, the person she called when she had a flat tire or had locked herself out of her place. Our place. I wanted us to live together and be a family. I wanted her to be Summer's stepmother. But I didn't know if she was up for that. I was going to have a conversation with her when that woman crashed into her on the ski slope, knocking Evie off her feet and giving all of us a bit of a fright.

Then, when we were laughing about it later, talking about the couple and how sweet they were, the words just tumbled out by themselves. There was no ring, I didn't have a proper proposal worked out. I wasn't even on my knees, looking my most handsome self. It was what I'd been thinking about, being together with her, forever.

She'd said yes, we kissed and then she said.

"What about kids?"

"If you want, we can have three," I said.

"Not four?" she teased.

"Okay, four," I conceded.

She looked surprised and I shrugged. "What? I've had a change of heart."

"When?"

"I've got the money right, we can get a nanny for every one of them. If that is what you want."

Evie said, "I don't know what I want, though, right now, it definitely isn't babies, but in ten years' time? Who knows?"

"Then we take it as it comes," I said. "Life is too short," I said. "I don't want to live in a world that doesn't exist yet. I want to be here, in it, with you. Preferably with a ring on your finger that tells the world you're mine."

I took a bit of foil from the champagne bottle and twisted it into a ring.

"With this ring, I thee wed," I said jokingly, placing it on her finger.

"I hope you don't think that gets you out of a real ring and a big wedding," she said, looking at me sternly.

"Because I want the whole shebang," she said.

"Then you shall have it. Are we talking carriages, France or maybe a castle in Italy?"

"And at least 400 of our dearest and closest friends," she said with a smile, then leaning in to kiss me.

"Sounds terrific," I said with a big smile.

She held out her hand with the tin foil ring. "Isn't it beautiful?"

"Not as beautiful as you," I said, knowing it was a cliché but meaning every word.

She leaned over to kiss me and I held her face, to kiss her longer, and deeper.

"You're with me now kid, for good," I said.

"Best news ever," she said with a happy sigh, snuggling into my chest.

Bonus chapter

A FEW DAYS BEFORE THE wedding, I started getting cold feet.

In a bad way.

It wasn't that I didn't love Tate or didn't want to be with him. But there was so much stress surrounding the whole wedding day. Once the media had gotten wind of it, we had reporters wanting to cover the event, offering to pay us for coverage, as if that would change my mind. But Tate was somebody. He was a Silicon Valley darling, a tech entrepreneur who had struck it big and made billions with his app company. In addition, he was handsome and sexy, with a reputation as a bit of a daredevil, the kind of guy who preferred walking on tightropes between buildings to actually working in them. It didn't help that he was married before to a Hollywood stylist and that he raised their daughter as a single dad. It only made him seem more attractive and more of a story.

And who was I?

Evie Gerick, barely 23, fresh out of college. Working for Tate Sagarro was my first real job and now I was marrying him. What a story! But I didn't want to be a story, I wanted to be a girl marrying the man of my dreams, and for our day to be only about us.

"Why do you sound so glum?" my mother asked me earlier in the week on the phone. "Are you having wedding jitters?"

"Maybe," I said in a shaky voice.

"What happened?" She asked quickly.

"Did he hit you?"

"No, no, nothing like that!"

But my mother wouldn't stop. "Did he yell at you, did you have a fight?"

"No, we didn't have an argument."

My mother carried on without even listening to me, "You know, your aunt Desirée, my sister, almost didn't marry your uncle Alan because she found out the day before the wedding that he had invited his ex-girlfriend to the wedding. She was convinced he still carried a torch for her. And maybe she was right, because you know, that marriage didn't last."

"Didn't she run off with a ski instructor?" I asked, pulled into my mother's story despite myself.

"Yes, well, it wasn't meant to be, obviously," my mother said.

"It's nothing like that," I said again.

"Then what are you worried about?" My mother asked. "Is it the age thing?" Tate was fourteen years older than me and while he was a very attractive man now, I had to admit, seeing his father had given me pause. Someone told me all men turned into their fathers eventually, and Mr. Sagarro was a lovely man, but the way he combed his remaining hair over his shiny bald head didn't do much for his looks. The beer belly didn't help either. The thought of Tate turning into that... Ugh! No!

"Was he mean to you again?"

I'd told my mom how Tate had in the beginning of our relationship, spent some time ignoring me after we'd slept together. I had told her about the time we'd spent apart and how when we decided to try being together, things between us were special. And I believed him when he said he'd never been in love before, that it had scared him when he'd had feelings for someone for the first time in his life. After caring only about himself for a long time, it came as a shock to his system. Being vulnerable, allowing someone into your heart and head, that was big.

"I don't know," I said, miserable.

"It's all so much.

It didn't help that Tate was away all week for work, smoothing over a deal with a major national media network. Whenever I spoke to him, he sounded stressed and tense, and I didn't want to bother him with details about the wedding, and have him think maybe I was adding to his stress. But he had been the one who wanted to get married in the first place? I was happy for us to keep seeing each other, to stay engaged, and have a bit more time on my own in the city, finding my feet. Did I really want to be Mrs. Sagarro so quickly? It could wait, couldn't it?

My mother wasn't helping. She started telling me about a friend who'd been engaged for ten years before they called off the whole thing because she found out her fiancé was gay.

"Tate is definitely not gay," I said, annoyed. She was making things worse.

"How would you know?" my mother said. "Linda told me the sex was great and she never suspected a thing."

I didn't want to think of friends of my mother having "great" sex. Who knew what that entailed?

"It's okay, Mom," I said, "It's going to be okay."

But that evening Tate didn't call, just sending me a curt message to say he'd be back in time for the wedding.

I was staying in the house, keeping an eye on his daughter Summer, who was eleven going on twenty-one. We'd always been great friends, but was I ready to become a stepmother? It sounded horrible. Would I have to dress differently now, wear my hair up? Stepmothers were strict, weren't they? Was I going to start telling her to clean up her room? Shouting at her to stop swearing or be more respectful to us? I really hoped not.

I could barely sleep that night. Whenever I nodded off, I had memories of wedding dresses being torn and running in the rain. I didn't need a therapist to help me analyze those. I was beginning to feel worse and had to call in sick at work the next day.

"Wedding fever, huh?" the receptionist sniggered and I put down the phone, went straight to bed and fell asleep. I spent the day in bed and sometime during the night, I woke up disorientated, convinced someone was in bed with me. Another nightmare! I was about to start screaming when Tate said, "Shh...it's me."

"Tate!" I was so glad he was back. I felt his arms around me, holding me tightly.

"Are you okay?" He asked me, concern and love filling his voice.

"No," I admitted. "I'm freaking out about the wedding."

He laughed, "Shall we call it off?"

I was horrified, "What? And what about the caterers and the venue?"

"Who cares?" He said, "We'll pay them and that's that."

"And all the guests, what do we tell them?"

"Whatever we want," he said, kissing my nose. "We say the stars weren't aligned, or the timing wasn't right or your spiritual guru advised against it."

"I don't have a spiritual guru," I said, laughing now too.

"They don't know that!"

"You wouldn't mind calling it off?" I ask.

"I mind only about you," he said.

It was dark in the bedroom, I couldn't see his face, but I could smell him and feel him and I was utterly reassured by his presence. "I'm so glad you're back, I muttered, pressing my head against his chest.

"You sounded a bit off yesterday," he said. "I thought I should come back and check on you."

"I'm glad you did," I said. "It got a bit much. Someone from a TV channel called to ask if they could film the wedding for an entertainment channel? He said they would send helicopters anyway. I mean, for me, I'm nobody!"

"You are not nobody, Evie," he said. "You are the girl who stole my heart, who finally got one of the most eligible single men in Silicon

Valley. That is a story. Everybody wants to know how you did it. If it is a sex thing or something you do with your legs..."

"Stop," I was laughing now. But I knew what he meant.

"Besides," he said. "There will be security and remember, the reception is indoors. Nobody will be able to take photographs with gigantic lenses, hiding in the greenery or something."

"You're so calm about all this," I said in wonder. "I mean, I thought you'd hate the fuss too."

"I'm used to it," he said quietly. "When you are a well-known individual, they use you to sell stories, to get clicks. If there is no story, they make it up. Just denying it creates a content stream. You have no idea how much has been written about me."

Actually, I did. I had Googled him before working for him and then later, when we stopped seeing each other, I was always looking up his name on social media.

"None of that matters," he said quietly.

"Only you and me matter. What we have. If you want to cancel the wedding, I have no problem doing that. As long as we stay together, as long as we are still us."

"We'll always be us," I said. I was sure of that. This was one thing I had absolutely no doubt about.

In the end, we did get married that Saturday afternoon.

It was a day drenched in golden sunlight, the vineyards glowing in the warmth of the afternoon sun as I made my way down the aisle. When I saw Tate waiting for me at the top of the church, my heart was beating faster.

This was it. This was our moment.

No matter what happened in the future, no matter if we had fights about whose folks we were going to for Christmas or why he was late again from work or if he'd spent too much money on a new Porsche or whatever, we would always have this.

A moment of utter beauty.

An afternoon where time stood still as our friends and family looked at us, smiling, their hearts filled with love and happiness for us as we turned to each other, took each other's hand and whispered the words to forever like a key to unlock a magic future. Maybe I'd watched too many Hallmark movies but when Tate slipped the ring on my finger and said in a voice breaking with emotion, "With this ring, I thee wed..." tears started running down my face.

This was happiness.

Someone who wanted me for me, who saw me for the person I was. Not just the baby of my family, or the PA who was a spreadsheet wizard. He wanted to be with me for better or for worse, but mostly, forever. Someone who knew that love didn't always come packaged the way you thought it would. That it looked and felt different to everyone.

But that only made it better.

Love, in the end, is its own reward.

And it was more than enough.

～♀～

Enjoy what you read? Then you'll love Ruthless Billionaire!

Don't miss out!

Visit the website below and you can sign up to receive emails whenever Erica Frost publishes a new book. There's no charge and no obligation.

https://books2read.com/r/B-A-YRSV-FXPDF

Did you love *Billionaire Engagement*? Then you should read *Ruthless Billionaire*[1] by Erica Frost!

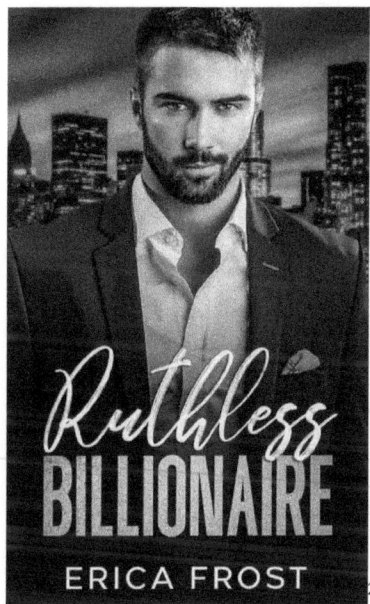

Falling for my ex's billionaire brother.

When I dated my ex, I loathed his older brother.

A bad-boy billionaire, Jesse Stanton seemed like the type to do anything for success.

Now, Jesse is being accused of murder.

And who does he ask for help?

Me. The girl he teased for being a goody two shoes.

Although I've only recently started working at the detective's office, solving crime is my passion.

I can't just stand by if there's even a tiny chance that Jesse is innocent.

---

1. https://books2read.com/u/49RA9d

2. https://books2read.com/u/49RA9d

Before long, I find myself sneaking around dark corners with him.

Pretending to be his girlfriend to get information.

I try to ignore Jesse's strong body, his sexy smirk, his irresistible eyes. All of this is fake, I tell myself.

Yet every fiber of my body hopes the billionaire is innocent of the crime.

And only guilty of stealing my heart.

Ruthless Billionaire is a standalone New Adult Romance with a HEA and NO cheating!

Also by Erica Frost

Seduced By A Billionaire
Dark Secrets
A Billionaire's Game
Power Play
Ruthless Rival
Taming The Billionaire
The Hated Billionaire
3-Pointer
Baby For The Billionaire
My Best Friend's Brother
Ruthless Rival
The Comeback
Billionaire Corruption
Nannying For A Billionaire
The Billionaire's Surprise Baby
Accidental Love
Billionaire Secrets
Ruthless Billionaire
Billionaire Engagement

Milton Keynes UK
Ingram Content Group UK Ltd.
UKHW031121081124
450926UK00001B/76

9 798224 384723